The
Gender
Trap

The Gender Trap

CHRIS JOHNSON & CATHY BROWN
WITH WENDY NELSON

PROTEUS
London & New York

PROTEUS BOOKS is an imprint of
The Proteus Publishing Group

United States
PROTEUS PUBLISHING CO., INC.
733 Third Avenue
New York, N.Y. 10017
distributed by:
THE SCRIBNER BOOK COMPANIES, INC.
597 Fifth Avenue
New York, N.Y. 10017

United Kingdom
PROTEUS (PUBLISHING) LIMITED
Bremar House,
Sale Place,
London, W2 1PT.

ISBN 0 906071 54 2

First published in 1982

Printed in Great Britain by The Anchor Press Ltd., and bound by
William Brendon & Son Ltd., both of Tiptree, Essex.

To Emma, in the hope that she will understand.

INTRODUCTION

I first met Chris Johnson and Cathy Brown in May 1980, when I was sent in pursuit of their story by the television company for which I work as a reporter and presenter. We struck up an immediate rapport, for in the confusion and uncertainty created by the Press' bombardment of the couple at that time, it was obvious that they needed understanding.

From the first it seemed totally natural to regard them as the man and woman they sought to be, so intrinsically did their actions and sensibilities disprove otherwise. During our initial meeting, Christ mentioned his desire to write about their unique experience and it seemed a logical step that we should utilize our friendship by joining together to write this book.

The story of Chris and Cathy is essentially a dual autobiography, for it is only together that they have achieved what both had individually longed for all their lives. However, the fact that it was two voices that needed to be heard, posed the problem of from whose viewpoint should their story be told and, after some careful deliberation, we all decided that this book should be written in the third person. Although for the early part of their lives they grew up entirely separate in widely differing circumstances, it is interesting to note that their transsexual convictions were nonetheless equally strong and just as equally stultified.

Because of the nature of their condition, which continues to defy all medical and scientific explanation, and their own self-analysis, Cathy and Chris felt it was vital to pass the knowledge they have gained onto a wider audience. The couple also realized that in ignorance of the true nature of transsexualism, it is all too easy to confuse this most unfortunate incongruity of body and mind with a whole range of unconventional sexual tendencies, and they felt that their autobiography would perhaps educate in this way. Between the three of us, therefore, our main aim has been to set the record straight about transsexualism and in so doing create a better understanding amongst those of us fortunate to have been born in the correct body, as well as giving support and reassurance to those who have not.

Viewing this unique story with a "modern" outlook can be a puzzling experience at first. In the past twenty years our traditional attitudes to human relationships, the roles in society of male and female, and sexuality have been set aside. In my early meetings with Chris and Cathy, I found it tempting time and again to wonder whether their course of action, involving radical medical treatment and surgery, wasn't over-extreme. Couldn't they find fulfilment and happiness simply by accepting that Anne was a dominant, career-minded and unmaternal woman? Or that Eugene was a rather passive, sensitive, even domesticated male?

But Chris and Cathy were adamant. Their predicament may not yet be fully understood by the doctors, but one thing seems clear: there is, and will always be a dividing line between enlightened sexual convention and the transsexual instinct.

In the course of writing it was interesting to discover that all of us found it difficult to consider the earlier lives of Anne and Eugene, so distasteful is that memory now and so far removed from their present sexual roles. For my own part, I hope that as a result of this book, Chris, Cathy and their daughter Emma are provided with some measure of financial support, for their chances of future employment are minimal and if surgery is further postponed through economic cuts to the social services in Britain, then costly private treatment will be their only alternative.

Wendy Nelson

ACKNOWLEDGEMENTS

Thanks are due to the following in the research and writing of this autobiography of Chris Johnson and Cathy Brown: Dr. Tim Betts, Tim Ward, May and Michael Brown, Edna Goldman, Solihull Maternity Hospital, Birmingham Evening Mail, Belfast City Library, Belfast Social Services Department and the Northern Ireland Office. Also to Skull, for her help in looking after Emma.

1

The timing could not have been worse. It was a weekend, and while Anne lay in hospital about to give birth, Eugene was caught between maintaining a constant vigil at her bedside and making what was to be his first live appearance on television. In a sense, it was the culmination of two of his dearest ambitions, yet now, both demands had to be met. The years of careful study, unbending self-discipline and application to the martial arts were finally being rewarded. So, it was in a state of feverish anticipation that he went on television to perform his Kung Fu exploits for the nation's children, who were glued to the popular Saturday morning show.

At an early age, Eugene had discovered an almost telepathic power within himself, in which he took refuge during his tough years at the Irish training school where he had been sent by the educational authorities after a long history of truancy. Naturally drawn to things mystical, this "power" had later led to a serious study of Chinese philosophy and, in particular, of the martial arts. His skill in this field gained him wide recognition, resulting finally in this televised demonstration.

His preoccupation with Anne's ordeal overshadowed any stagefright he might have felt at exhibiting his talents before such a large and unknown audience; for once he went through the motions almost mechanically. Even so it was still impressive and the children loved it.

Afterwards it was not congratulations, mutual back-slapping and hospitality that he wanted, but to get away to the hospital as fast as was possible. The show's producer obliged.

I remember what a funny little chap he was; he was incredible on the show but he was in a hell of a state. He said something about his wife being about to have a baby any minute and he had to get there, fast. He was panicking because he hadn't got any transport – in fact he said he couldn't drive – so I ran him over there.'

As it happened, there was no immediate rush, for Anne's labour was to be painful and protracted. If she had managed to avoid facing up to the reality of her situation over the past nine months, its full impact was now, as she expected, brought home to her in no uncertain terms. The moment she had long dreaded had arrived and as she lay in pain, so her physical suffering was deepened by the mixed thoughts and feelings racing through her head.

There was no question of she and Eugene marrying. Even though Anne had long separated from her husband, Andrew, and divorce was merely a matter of time, to re-marry knowing full well that generically the bride should have been the bridegroom and vice versa would have been, although legal, a travesty. It would have to be discounted, and while both of them regretted the fact, they felt secure enough in their commitment to each other for it not to be unduly worrying.

Far more perturbing was the ludicrousness of living in abject confusion of mind and identity. Here was a man longing to be a woman, loving a woman who yearned to be a man. They had tried for hours to work out a solution. There seemed to be no one to whom they could go for advice, for fear of being thought of as abnormal and somewhat perverted.

Instead, Anne turned to books, gleaning what she could from a library of psycho-analysis and philosophy. Often it led nowhere but self-analysis had of course been part of her training as a social worker and the more that she and Eugene could examine their motives the better.

Whatever else was undecided, she now had a label, a name tag to live by and one which both were agreed was at last appropriate. They were transsexuals, a term which was still excluded from many of the minor dictionaries.

It defies a neat definition, the essence being that a transsexual holds the irrational but firm belief that he or she has been born within the wrong body and is therefore of the wrong gender and sex.

It's a sad reflection on the human race that man, for all his endless circumspection, has never come to grips with just why there are transsexuals. Their problem remains largely misunderstood and more often than not, misinterpreted.

For in ignorance it is easy to correlate transsexual with transvestite, with bisexual or homosexual, all paths which the pair had considered but rejected.

None of them was applicable; true, Eugene enjoyed wearing feminine clothes and Anne had shown a preference for male garb for most of her life: but neither dressed up for sexual gratification, as does the transvestite, but more as a natural manifestation of their respective inner personae. Although physically of one sex, they were psychologically of another, and both knew that this was so.

Homosexuality was an option Eugene had always found abhorrent. Feeling as he did a confirmed female, he could no more imagine making love man to man than he could share his bed with another woman. Only Anne, for obvious reasons, was acceptable. Only bisexualism seemed at all appropriate, given Anne's ability to love and marry a man and her subsequent affections for other women.

On examination even that was a poor analogy, for in her husband Andrew she had sought a comfort and security which she could now analyse as similar to that of a young boy, clinging almost innocently to a full grown and interesting man. As for her women friends, they were easily explained now that she fully recognized her own masculinity.

The term then, to which both she and Eugene felt themselves best suited was transsexual and it was gratifying to know that their predicament had been scientifically recognized, if subsequently virtually ignored.

The odds of two transsexuals not only meeting but falling in love must be tiny indeed, but for Anne and Eugene it was unbelievable good fortune: that each could share their dilemma with the other, knowing it would be fully appreciated and understood, as by no other person.

Their quest then, was to be a joint venture of spirit and of heart and one which they were convinced could not be put off a moment longer. For now they had come this far, there could be no further compromise, no returning to the falsehood they had both lived with for so long. In the hours of thought and often of argument, the one overriding problem remained unaltered: that their physical make-up was at odds with their

13

innermost feeling. It was only by changing themselves physically that they could hope to be truly in unison, and to become wholesome, complete entities.

Meanwhile, so strong was the transsexual impulse, that Eugene found himself experiencing strong and impulsive urges which he could not explain. He began to suffer periodic and unashamed broodiness, an insistent need to have a child which could not be denied.

Many women of childbearing age would identify with his mood: a maternal instinct that no man could ever fully understand. Yet there he was, longing for his dream to come true, yet knowing that a mother was something he could never hope to become.

This was one tender point with which Anne found it hard to sympathize.

'I had never felt like it in my life, it was an instinct I could not grasp at all. The whole idea of having children had always been abhorrent to me, I didn't want to know.'

But in spite of himself Eugene started to nag; however unreasonable the demand, he wanted to have a child so badly that somehow he would have to be fulfilled.

Life as transsexuals meant taking on impossible complications and hoping to stagger through. Already, they were being thrown into much deeper water than they had ever anticipated. They had to make a decision; and so it was, after a great deal of careful thought, that they drew up the plan.

Most of us have hopes of some imperceptible scheme in life, of a logical progression that will bring us happiness and fulfilment but which rarely sticks to its course and is often the better for it. None of us though, has had to contemplate following the fantastic plan of action which Anne and Eugene now prepared for themselves. It remains in all probability unique and its final strength has yet to be tested.

Nonetheless, it was a brave and daring scheme that would demand great courage to complete. In the event, both knew that there was no real alternative and so the decision was made to begin straightaway.

What they had in mind may have sounded irrational even to some little short of irresponsible, but it was equally inevitable if they were to achieve their dearest ambitions.

They had to change sex, to somehow transform themselves

physically if they were to transcend the bodies they had been born with. From the vague knowledge Anne had managed to gather, that would involve lengthy and unpalatable medical treatment, eventual surgery and all the heartache and pain which that implied. Moreover, it would demand an unwavering determination to succeed, for psychologically they would be entering the realms of the unknown as they passed through an androgynous and probably prolonged period of being physically neither one thing nor the other.

Yet before they embarked on this course there was a further drastic consideration; for once hormone treatment began they would both be rendered impotent, Eugene unable to father a child or Anne to conceive. Nor, given that they succeeded in their sex changes, Anne becoming male, Eugene a female, would either have the necessary internal equipment for reproduction. Either way, having children of their own would be out of the question.

To Anne this was of little consequence, devoid as she was of maternal instincts; for Eugene though, it was an unbearable flaw in what was otherwise a perfect scheme.

Part two of the plan then, was in many ways far more difficult and preposterous than the first. If they were to conceive at all, it would have to be now, with Eugene fathering Anne's baby. It is difficult to imagine just how repulsive this was to Anne. She had never entertained the idea of pregnancy; it was so alien to her nature that she had dismissed it from her life as something she would never have to face. Now it was unavoidable, for once they had begun the changeover even adoption would be out of the question.

'With our background no agency would want to entrust a child to us, it would've been unrealistic to imagine they would. The only way was to have a child of our own and we wanted to be together so very badly that for Eugene's sake I had to make that sacrifice.'

After all, she reasoned with herself, what was nine months if it opened the way to a whole new life together?

'It's a strange analogy, but it was a bit like going to the dentist; it's painful and unpleasant, but you grin and bear it because you know that in the end the results will be worth all the effort − not that I ever relished going to the dentist!'

Anne had been taking the pill as a form of birth control for eight or nine years, since her first sexual encounter. She had expected that it would take some time for her body to readjust and for the effect of the hormones to disperse from her system; it seemed unlikely that she would conceive quickly.

To her horror and amazement and to Eugene's delight, it happened immediately.

'As the dates eventually worked out, it must've been about a week later. In any case it all happened before I'd had a chance to think twice.'

It was the end of April, the baby would arrive shortly after Christmas and the remainder of 1976 was to be the most unnatural period of her life.

'Remembering it now I can only see it through a haze, a mist. Because it was just about the ultimate admission of womanhood I could make, it was as if I tried to blank it out, to imagine that it wasn't really me who was pregnant at all; that way I could accept it, put on a brave face and somehow get through.'

Now, in the hospital, no one but Eugene had any idea of the appalling battle raging inside this particular young expectant mother. No doctor was aware that his patient felt little more of a woman than the men around her, and that as they prodded and probed, she was suffering a hundredfold the indignity of giving birth. For it was tantamount to asking any man to experience childbirth, a notion he would undoubtedly find quite alien. Anne was no exception.

For the first three months of pregnancy, it had been quite easy to overlook what was happening to her. She was in good health and there were no outward physical signs to betray the fact that she was expecting.

However, as her body began to change and grow large, so the conflict between mind and body became unbearable.

She felt cumbersome and incongruous, the pride of expectancy sitting ungraciously on her.

'Most pregnant mothers look awkward and uncomfortable, but I looked terrible, completely out of shape and entirely unnatural. I felt like an elephant, I had no idea how to carry myself and I had no intention of bothering to learn. In fact I was never totally aware of the baby growing inside me – I tried to ignore it as much as possible – there was simply no question of having any pride in myself, certainly no joy at what was happening to me.'

So deep was her embarrassment at the great concern shown to her by colleagues, that work became increasingly difficult to face each morning.

'It's that special regard that people seem to have for pregnant women – be careful, don't lift that, how are we today dear? – They were all very well meaning but I couldn't stand it. The last thing I wanted was to be treated like a precious little woman, doing her bit to keep the population going.'

To make matters worse, other women in the department were also pregnant:

'They regarded me as a comrade, as if all we wanted to do was to make baby talk.'

Anne found it utterly distasteful, but as luck would have it an old cartilage trouble flared up again making it extremely painful to walk; she was laid off work until it improved. The rest from the office benevolence was such a great relief that Anne found the idea of returning unbearable. Better to withdraw as soon as possible. If others wanted to rejoice in her giving birth, then all well and good, so long as they did not expect her to share in the enthusiasm.

After some persuasion and several telephone conversations, it was agreed that Anne be allowed to break her three-year contract and leave the social services at once. Even so, it was galling to give up the job she so enjoyed, but until she was rid of her intolerable burden she would have no peace.

But what of Eugene? Similarly, the enormity of their situation was proving increasingly frustrating for him as his initial delight at Anne's conception lapsed into a base and incorrigible jealousy which, although he tried, he could barely suppress.

Thankful though he was for Anne's tremendous self-sacrifice, thrilled at the prospect of becoming a parent, he longed for the change to feel an embryo developing inside him, to experience for himself all that she was going through. It was a tortuous craving that became totally absorbing as the pregnancy went on, for the maternal instincts Eugene knew to be so much a part of him were now making themselves felt.

From the first he was fascinated by the pregnancy: 'If I couldn't physically be its mother, I could be in spirit. I could feel the anticipation, the anxiety, the overawing delight, even the twinges. I wanted to absorb it all and remember it forever.'

As they lay in bed together those autumn and winter nights,

17

the baby kicking impatiently inside her womb, Anne felt only a numb despair, a sense of detachment. Eugene, sensing the involuntary movements, snuggling close to hear not one lone heartbeat but two, found himself outraged.

'I couldn't describe how frustrated I was, I'd never felt so angry and upset. What I could feel and hear should've been going on inside me, it should've been happening to me!'

At the hospital bedside, Eugene was proffering support and comfort as best he could, both with the mechanics of contractions and breathing and with the more intangible agonies that Anne was having to endure. Now that the birth was imminent he too was in a highly nervous state; worried for Anne, envious for himself.

'I felt that I was going crazy in there, completely off my head. I played the nurses up merry hell, I wouldn't leave Anne when they wanted me out, it was just terrible.'

Ostensibly, he was playing to perfection the part of the overanxious expectant father; in fact, his neurosis was more to do with despair at witnessing the women, each so intent on the intimate task of delivering her child. It was something of an exclusive club in which Eugene was only tolerated so long as he fulfilled the part of supportive partner.

No wonder then, that those last few months provoked arguments which neither had anticipated, for as a means to an end it had proved to be a nightmare which neither wanted to relive under any circumstances.

There was, of course, the necessity for periodical medical attention, for Anne to visit the ante-natal clinic run weekly for all expectant mothers. The classes were not compulsory, but doctors frowned on those who chose not to attend. In any case, at twenty-seven, Anne was not a young woman as far as pregnancy was concerned; it was better to play safe than to be sorry.

If her colleagues' solicitude had been overpowering, then this was to prove infinitely worse. To lie on the floor amidst a sea of prone, heavily pregnant women, practising unwieldy exercises for that most horrifying fundamental experience of birth was, she told herself, the final indignity. She had temporarily overlooked the eventual need to give birth; right then that hardly warranted contemplation.

By way of offering some moral support, Eugene often went

along with her, to share in the experience as much as possible. Indeed, when the instruction became more specific and the class was shown a film of childbirth it was Anne who ducked out, horrified by the blood and guts scenario, while Eugene sat entranced along with the rest of the women.

It was an inordinately testing time, the monotony of being at home all day made Anne grow increasingly irritable and for the first time the almost idyllic tone of their love was tempered by arguments and frequently bitter rows.

If the discussion was not over the existence of God – and this had become something of an overriding preoccupation – then it was usually concerned with money. For when Anne gave up her job they became dependent on Eugene as the breadwinner, a difficult enough responsibility given his up-bringing in which the tendency had always been to live very much from hand to mouth. In his present state of agitation it became even more impossible to cope with, and unknown to Anne he began to borrow money. It was never much at a time, small sums just to tide them over, but gradually the number of people to whom they were in debt reached unmanageable proportions.

Many of them were people whom Anne had never heard of, casual acquaintances Eugene had met through the martial arts; it became less and less likely that they would all be repaid.

'He would never come clean with me and tell me what was going on financially, I just didn't know where we stood. I found it so exasperating to know that I couldn't control the situation any more. Andrew and I had never been well off, but we'd at least always known where our next meal was coming from; now I had to depend on Eugene and that just wasn't on.'

Their financial headache did nothing to improve Eugene's general mental state: he became fidgety and nervous and as the pregnancy progressed he grew more deeply disturbed. More than anything else it seriously disrupted his powers of concentration, so that retaining his grip on the Kung Fu school became a continual struggle.

'As my self-confidence deteriorated so I got more strict with my pupils and I'd blow up at the slightest thing. It was just awful but there was no way I could stop, the pressure was far too great.'

Anne could no longer take an active part in classes but she

enjoyed being a spectator and welcomed the chance to keep in touch with her friends. The change in Eugene and in the couple's relationship did not go unnoticed, especially by Tim Ward, the proprietor of the school where Eugene taught Kung Fu.

'He'd changed a lot had Eugene, and at one point I felt that he was very mixed up, as if he'd become almost imbalanced in some way.

'We'd have the inevitable tussle over money and I realized they were in difficulties. In any event they began to row together quite a lot; I felt that Anne was the quiet force behind the throne so to speak. I don't know if it was because of the baby or what, but Eugene certainly seemed to have lost some of his old sparkle.'

Nonetheless, the pair still showed their mutual affection, as Liz, a friend from the days of the martial arts school, remembers:

'Eugene would come over as I was chatting to Anne, and put his arm around her. She was never very happy wearing smocks, but he'd comfort her, put his hand on her lump and give it a little pat, as if to show me how pleased he was. I thought it was quite touching.'

As the baby's arrival became imminent, so the tension worsened, but no one could have guessed at the true depths of their exasperation; for by and large they appeared to be a normal, moderately happy couple experiencing the usual worries over having their first child.

All along there had been the additional worry of Anne's family, and their reaction to her becoming pregnant by a man who was not her husband, with a baby who would therefore be illegitimate.

'Naturally they were shocked and not particularly happy at the news; it was hard for them to take when I'd had no children with Andrew. They'd aways assumed that I was something of a career person.'

Throughout the nine long months they had shown little interest in her well-being, rather a cold hostility which, while understandable, Anne found more upsetting than she cared to admit at the time.

So Anne and Eugene's second Christmas together was hardly comparable with the first, Anne feeling wretched and grossly misshapen as she endured the final miserable few days before the birth. If relatives had shown a certain coolness over the event, in material terms they were nothing but supportive. So generous were they that the couple found themselves inundated with every essential of nursery paraphernalia, supposedly vital to the survival of a newly-born babe. There was little need for them to make any lengthy shopping trips in preparation, although that was something Eugene enjoyed. If their baby was to be born into unique circumstances, materially it would want for nothing. Throughout, both had hoped fervently that the baby would be a girl. For Anne it would be an unbearable irony to produce a boy and she felt certain that her jealousy would be too great for her to live with. So maintaining his faith in God, Eugene and even Anne, resorted to the power of prayer, in desperate hope that they would be answered in the shape of a baby daughter.

'We prayed so hard that somehow we just knew that was what it'd turn out to be, we were really in no doubt about that at all.'

With the New Year their interminable wait was finally over; January was only nine days old when Anne went into labour and found herself in that most sacrosanct of female preserves, the local Solihull maternity hospital. So the moment she had long dreaded had arrived and if pregnancy was tortuous, then she expected what she was about to face to be sheer purgatory.

As the loathsome hours ticked away, the pain growing more wearisome, so Anne's distraction grew. It was almost as though, in some incomprehensible way, her reluctance to become a mother was being reflected in the lengthy delay, so that whilst the mind remained unwilling, so somehow the flesh remained weak.

Even the eventual epidural injection, administered to dull the pain while allowing her to feel the sensation of childbirth, proved uncomfortable. (The marks remain prominent to this day.) Anne felt starvingly hungry: two pieces of toast in thirty-six hours was hardly enough to sustain her. Her health would be at risk if the baby did not come soon, and medical opinion was one of concern. Strangely this gave Anne a fresh hope; all along she had prayed fervently that she would not have to give birth via the usual channel; that the ultimate intimacy of a natural childbirth as the baby was expelled was something she would never know.

21

In the event, her prayers were answered. It became obvious that after a day and a half in labour, Anne would have to undergo a Caesarian section. No one was surprised at her relief.

So, on January 11, 1977, Anne and Eugene were delivered of a daughter on the operating table. A baby girl, tiny and jaundiced, and with a mop of dark hair and slant eyes, looking distinctly oriental. The worst was surely over, the baby a living portent of their new life together.

2

Experience had taught both Anne and Eugene to be sceptical of portent. Twenty-eight years earlier, in 1949 (the year of Anne's birth), had been a time when Britain certainly felt Great. Post-war austerity was more than outweighed by the optimism for a peaceful future, the country concerned with regaining the stability which to a great extent stemmed from the sound social basis of family life. The baby boom of which both Anne and Eugene, born the year before, were a part, sent councils into a frenzy of activity for the preparation of extra welfare and schooling for the bulging population.

That Royalty set the example with an infant prince, closely followed by a curly-haired princess, was seized upon by the media as an omen of an assured and happy future. To be born then was to be fortunate indeed. For were not these the babes whose freedom the nation had been fighting for? Man the provider, the protector, had fought his battles and now was intent on working his hardest to support his growing offspring. Woman, thriving on the challenge of building a home for her loved ones, knew with certainty that the sky was blue and free of buzz bombs. Relieved, she abandoned the forces, farm or munitions factory and revelled in the joys of motherhood. Secure in their roles, young parents instilled in their children the bravery of manhood, the gentle patience of a woman.

No one doubted that pink was for a girl, blue for a boy. And as guaranteed by no fewer than twelve Royal babies of late, the new generation sucked its canned baby milk and grew plump and content as never before.

Britain was in the grip of a relentless heatwave and the signs augered well for a sweltering Bank Holiday.

The one preoccupation in the land-locked Midlands was escape, by whatever means, to the fresh sea air. The industrial fortnight, when the region's factories stood uniformly idle, held such promise that the crowds for the coast trains at Birmingham's New Street station stood four deep, and six thousand holidaymakers spent the night under the stars at Liverpool docks, so great was the demand for the Isle of Man ferry.

For those marooned at home there were Sunshine Follies in the parks or *Perchance to Dream* and *Blue Lagoon* at theatre and cinema. Despite the heat a crowd of thirty five thousand crammed the Molyneux soccer ground at Wolverhampton to hear Churchill bemoan the dollar gap and the inevitable resultant unemployment.

By Monday July 25, milk, sweets, and cigarettes, already rationed, were in severely short supply at the south coast resorts. As pavements melted in the afternoon temperature of eighty four degrees, Birmingham Assize judge Mr. Justice Streatfield took the unprecedented step of pronouncing "wigs off" in the Divorce Court division. At the HP sauce factory, deserted for the holiday, Aston Villa soccer team, training for the new season, were among the few who did not welcome the blistering heat.

Such was the day of Anne Johnson's birth. The new daughter of a Birmingham metal polisher, she was welcomed as an afterthought to a family already well-established with three adolescent children, a girl and two boys. The age gap between the youngest child and the new baby girl was exactly ten years. Cosseted, loved by all from the moment of her arrival on that boiling July holiday, Anne was delivered at home into the security of suburbia; to thrive under the loving care of parents who were thrilled by the promise of their darling daughter.

By contrast, the previous spring in Northern Ireland had been unseasonally cold when, only two hours after being wheeled into the labour ward at Armagh's Tower Hill Hospital, May Brown was delivered of a son.

Weighing in at just under nine pounds, the boy was nonetheless put into an incubator to relieve what May recalls as his inordinate cracked and wrinkled pinkness.

A week later she said goodbye to the maternity wing and stood alone at the hospital gate – her baby strapped close, shawled heavily against the flurrying snowstorms that had surprised Armagh that spring. So laden, May watched the traffic crawl by, impatient at the inclement weather.

She made her way to the bus stop and so it was that bundled on board, jammed against the morning shoppers, May's baby began his first journey in life. It was a humble homecoming to the lodging house that was currently May's home. The year or so since she had met her baby's father, Eugene, she had spent mostly alone.

That day was no exception, her husband serving His Majesty's Pleasure in the Crumlin Road jail for some indiscreet petty thieving. Not that May expected support; the daughter of a mill girl – her father had died when she was eight – life had always rollercoasted from good to bad.

Leaving her mother to the arms of a fruit dealer in Newtown, May had adventured her way to Belfast via a colourful path; working the land through the war years, housekeeping for the clergy of the Church of Ireland and eventually joining the circus, where she perfected an accomplished song and dance act. On meeting and falling in love with Eugene Brown she had become part of an inveterate band of Irish travellers who wandered the Province as fancy and where prospects took them. Living on the road, surviving where they could by collecting and selling discarded clothing, it was more by accident than design that their baby's birthplace was Armagh.

In a matter of weeks the child, already used to accompanying his mother on the daily collecting round, was packed tightly into his straw cradle – a gift from May's girlfriend – and bussed the forty odd miles to the capital city.

The family united for the first time, the young boy was named Eugene, in honour of his father.

However, right from the start, Eugene's life was highly unpredictable; home was wherever the word had it that pickings were good and thus the family was always on the move, rarely settling in one place for more than a week at a time. In this fashion they travelled the circuit from Belfast to Dundalk, then east and north to Dungannon and Portadown, lodging up a variety of backstairs, scraping a living that never left them hungry but rarely made them comfortable.

But if the little boy grew quick and wily beyond his years, his sense of morality was more than catered for by the embrace of the Catholic church. While May had been brought up in the

25

tradition of the Church of Ireland, Eugene was pure southern Irish Catholic stock and their son was baptized into the Catholic faith. Not that the Browns were overtly religious; their attendances at Mass were sporadic and more from a sense of duty than fervour. Nevertheless Eugene's early knowledge of the Church was Catholicism at its most dogmatic. The catechism and confessional and the fear of retribution instilled by the priests and the more devout Catholics Eugene met as they meandered from village to town became an unwritten code for him to live by. By the age of four this lone child had developed a whimsical approach to life that marked him out from his contemporaries. Unable to build up any stable relationships or friendships by the very nature of his haphazard existence, Eugene became his own best friend, and as often with any only child, he developed a vivid and imaginative world of his own.

'I used to daydream, perhaps you'd say no more than most children. But I can remember very clearly, simply knowing with some certainty that there must be something beyond what was going on all around me.

'At first I had dreams of all sorts of happenings and events, fascinating things, like a vision, like bombs going off inside my head. It happened quite frequently. I'd be absorbed in something else when suddenly flash! I'd click into it. Then suddenly it'd all be gone.'

By the time Eugene was ready for school, the "visions" had become more apparent.

'I never got anywhere at school because of them – I couldn't concentrate for long on writing or reading without things flashing before me, clicking me off from what was really happening. You can put it down to imagination, but what I saw was real enough to me to stay vivid even now.

'It always happened unconsciously too. I remember a shop – it was called Drakes – it was closed and I was hanging around by the window. There was a little hole so tiny I knew it was impossible, but I wondered what would happen if I put my hand through. I wouldn't have stolen anything because I knew that wasn't right, but I could feel myself pushing and willing myself to try and do what looked impossible. Quite suddenly my hand was through. It was incredible. I don't know what I did.'

This self-awareness may not seem particularly unusual, but

four-year-old Eugene secretly dubbed it his "power", a sensitivity he was to develop and draw on as he grew. This apart, the boy was by nature a loner, but the children he did meet and shared classrooms with, eventually found him friendly and fun. The ability to laugh at life was something he had learned from May, who long ago had realized the value of a sense of humour in her often dire straits. The two spent much of their time together, the errant but nonetheless lovable Mr. Brown spasmodically disappearing for a spell in jail. The bond of mother and son was strong.

If Eugene was a particularly affectionate child and demonstrably so, May was delighted to find comfort and support from her little one.

'Right from the first day at school he didn't settle. He hated it, having to sit and concentrate. An hour'd pass and I'd be busying myself when I'd hear his school bag drop on the floor. He'd come home – or rather time and again so I found out, he'd never been near the school at all, he'd just wandered up and down the street till it was too late.'

For Eugene there was more happiness and contentment to be found in trailing his mother on her collection, or in escaping to the fantasy world of make believe that is the natural play of childhood, but which Eugene enjoyed above all else.

'Even as a tot he'd be clumping around in my stilettos,' says May. 'Dressing up, well he just loved it, he was always raiding my wardrobe.'

As for toys, Eugene was fickle. He did not have many, but one Christmas his big surprise from Santa Claus was a profound disappointment.

'It was a Roy Rogers' cowboy kit, the complete works, gun, holster and all. I really was disappointed and I remember I upset them all by bursting into tears. I'd really hoped I was going to have a doll.'

His only faithful toy was a bedraggled golliwog, which accompanied Eugene the length and breadth of Ulster for nine turbulent years.

So the weeks and months past, the boy's education irregular and very distasteful to him. If May was worried at her son's lack of schooling, she tried to ignore her guilt, excusing it as inevitable given the life they had to lead.

But if Eugene seemed fey and wayward it was not simply his

family life or his hatred of school that made him detached from his peers.

For as well as the "power" that gave him such inspired but troubling thoughts, Eugene held a conviction that would overwhelm the most stable among us in its outrageousness.

Certainly for a child of the early Fifties it was a realization he could never confide, even to his adoring mother.

By the time he was five years old, Eugene Brown knew with profound certainty that he was not a boy.

'Everyone told me I was, of course, and physically I looked like all the other boys. But in my head I just knew there was something very wrong. I didn't feel like a boy, no matter what I seemed.'

Where that astounding thought came from, no one knows. To have told of this innermost feeling would only have invited ridicule and dismissal as an overworked childish imagination.

In any case, if he was not a young male how he could be in any shape or form a female was a detail Eugene had not then figured out.

'All I knew was that I didn't feel like a boy, I didn't want to act like one and didn't want to be one.'

With this realization, Eugene withdrew more determinedly into himself. Firmly convinced that he was different, he took delight in his apparent ability to read the minds of others.

'It was like a radio, as if I could hear people speaking without them moving their lips, I knew what they were thinking.

'If I had any enemies among the other kids, I'd know if they were planning to get me and I'd work out something a hundred times worse to do to them.'

This childish malevolence nurtured a more harmful rebelliousness, so that by the time he was ten, Eugene was determined to fight the world that had made him what he was. The one diversion from this delinquent path was the arrival of his brother, Michael.

'He adored that baby, he'd rock him and cuddle him and help me all he could,' says May.

But if helping with Michael took his mind off things, it was also a grand excuse for skipping school.

'I made the most of it. While the folks were away out on the road I'd take the day off and look after him. It was a relief to

Mum and I liked it, carrying Michael around everywhere. I'd feed him and change him, just like Mum did. In a way, I s'pose, I was more of a little mother to him than she was, the amount of time we spent together.'

But if Eugene was happy with this arrangement, the Northern Ireland school inspectorate was certainly not. After four letters of apologetic excuse for his absence, the man from the school would descend, quizzing the Browns as to why their son had repeatedly missed school. Unable to come up with valid enough reasons, the inspector would file his report and sternly admonish one and all for their constant failure to comply with the law.

For the Browns, getting Eugene to take learning seriously was like fighting the proverbial losing battle.

His attitude towards the formality and strictures of Catholic schooling had hardened with adolescence, to the point where even the authorities questioned whether he would ever conform.

'All they concentrated on was maths, English and religion. It was boring and dogmatic – we weren't allowed to question anything. I got impatient and angry with them. There had to be more to life than their one-sided, narrow view. I really couldn't see the point.'

This attitude, combined with their unpredictable existence, meant more often than not all the Browns' good intentions led to nothing and Eugene would miss days and often weeks of term time.

Astute, and with a natural sense of survival, he found the reality of life on the road a continuous adventure, far richer in experience than endless weeks in the schoolroom.

If he was a rebel, Eugene was not a strong child. As he reached puberty, a wheezing bronchial condition that made it difficult for him to breathe became so bad that May took him to Belfast's Royal Hospital, where doctors advised he see a psychiatrist. While they could find nothing physically wrong, Eugene was pronounced to have a nervous, slightly asthmatic, condition.

What was causing him worry, no one asked. Eugene would not tell, and so the all absorbing doubts the boy had about his gender remained secret, stored subconsciously at the back of his young mind.

They were to be abruptly awakened on a chill autumn day as

Eugene wandered aimlessly through Brown Square in the centre of Belfast. He was fourteen and the pattern of dodging the school board had continued with such monotonous regularity that their patience had run out.

Three months previously, his father had been threatened with a warrant for his arrest for failing to send Eugene to school. The family had slipped over the border to the sanctuary of an uncle who lived in a remote village on the faraway western shores of County Clare: and there they had stayed until gauging it safe to return to Belfast.

The traditional luck of the Irish was never in evidence when the Browns were in need of it. Their assessment as to when their return would pass unnoticed was plainly optimistic. So it was that a particularly astute policeman, patrolling the square that autumn day, watched with interest the lad kicking stones with such feeling. After the customary approach he recognized Eugene and promptly took him into custody. Eugene was confined for two days, resilient to all questions and uncooperative in his anger.

He was taken before the Juvenile Court, a sombre chamber empty except for a handful of interested parties. He listened passively as the social worker recommended that, in view of the circumstances, it was felt to be in his best interest to be taken out of parental control and detained in the care of the court.

Bewildered and in panic, Eugene fell back on the full fury of his Irish temper. But it was no use. Yelling abuse, he was led to a waiting police car and driven away, his freedom abruptly curtailed.

Eugene's first glimpse of the place he was to know as home for the next three years filled him with a cold fear. Standing imposingly at the end of the Glen Road, the school was secured from the mainstream of Belfast life by an imposing hedge of barbed wire.

Bewildered, he was led through a labyrinth of locked doors and corridors, every pane of door or window reinforced with tough steel wire. Eventually he found himself in a small office, where he was stripped both of his clothing and his identity. From now on Eugene Brown Jnr was to be known only as number 121.

The head of this austere establishment was Brother Adrian,

a remote figure who was aided in his task of disciplining the unruly young Catholics by an entourage of trainee priests. They demanded unquestioning obedience and respect from their charges, and showed no hesitation in wielding brute force where they met ignorance.

'What faith I ever had in the Catholic church was utterly destroyed by those men. They saw us as having the Devil in us, but as to showing us any sort of Christian charity, well, they were plain hypocritical. They seemed to think the only way to keep us down was to be ruthless and violent. I hated and despised them right from the start.'

Eugene's clothes and toilet things were labelled and numbered; he was taken to a dormitory in the senior block.

'There were six or seven other boys sleeping in there. One of them was the head boy, he was sort of in charge. They were curious to find out about me, but I quickly decided I was going to keep myself to myself as much as I could. I knew that was the best way to survive.'

The strict timetable meant that the day began with Mass at the unseemly hour of five thirty. Dazed by lack of sleep, the boys would mumble through offertory and benediction before breakfast, served in relays and announced by a burst of shrill whistles.

Most of Eugene's fellow inmates were in for "breaking", a few for sexual assaults such as rape.

Cooped up, restless and frustrated, they vented their youthful energies on petty rivalries, often with cruel results.

'There were the bullies, of course. I couldn't swim so I'd get thrown in. In the end, I managed to learn, thank God. But there was one little fat fellow – Daley his name was – he was terrified of water. He'd scream with fear. These two louts got him and they threw him in the deep end. He was bobbing up and down and gulping for breath. I couldn't do anything, I couldn't swim well enough. Anyway, he disappeared three times before one boy eventually dived in and fished him out. Not that it did him any good; he just got belted for saving Daley's life.'

Beltings and beatings, with the cane or steel ruler, were a common occurrence for number 121. If he had resisted schooling before, this Belfast training school made his defiance more obdurate.

'I went along to the lessons, but I just refused to work, point blank. I didn't see why I was in there in the first place, and I wasn't going to let them get the better of me, no way.'

Simple insubordination, such as failing to address a priest as sir or brother, warranted punishment. Outright disobedience, as shown by 121, met with more.

'If you really got on their nerves you'd go before the Brothers' Committee and then they'd use the cat o'nine tails or a strip of hard leather.'

The ultimate threat was the cells, dark secured rooms below the cookhouse.

'I remember one boy with red hair and big staring eyes. He was always down in the cells cooling off for something or other, hitting a brother or refusing to do jobs.'

But for Brown 121 there were even worse problems. Enclosed societies of young men are a recognized breeding ground for homosexuality and it was not long before homosexual approaches were made to Eugene.

'Because I was small and fit and not bad looking they all assumed I was a queer. I just found it repulsive and I refused to give in to them. But it made my life hell.'

So it was that one night after lights out, six boys determined to call 121's bluff. Pouncing as a gang on his sleeping figure, they began to strip him of pyjamas, pulling him down into an uncompromising position. But they had reckoned without Eugene's wiry strength. Before they had a chance to molest him he was on the defensive.

'I was furious. Frightened too, but I was so angry I just lunged out and grabbed one of them by the head and squeezed as hard as I could. I was shouting "I'll kill you" and he was going red and then purple with choking.

'If someone hadn't run for the housemaster I'd have strangled him for sure.'

Eugene had managed to save himself from the embarrassment of being molested, but his unpopularity plummeted to new levels when the entire dormitory was subsequently put on report. The monthly Sunday pass was stopped for four months as punishment, and Brown 121 was caned for his violent throttling.

'After that, well they were all gunning for me. They'd spit on my bread so I couldn't eat it, and then when I refused to gulp it down, two of the brothers would have me and give me a banging.'

On one occasion and in desperation the brothers marched him outside to the middle of the yard, to stand there until he agreed to comply.

Loath to give in, 121 stood frozen through the night. In the morning he was put on report and taken to the cells to cool off.

But the taunts and provocation clearly did not work. Disinterested in the usual healthy outlet of football, an unwilling if efficient goalkeeper at hurley, Eugene chose to express his personal fury by remaining sullen and aloof. Unrepentant and unbroken, he firmly refused to participate in school and was dismissed from the classroom to the laundry.

At last he was to find some relief from the overbearing dominance of the all-male society he had come to detest so much. The laundry was in the capable hands of a nun, one Mother Ignatius, who cared for the needs of boys and brotherhood alike.

To Eugene, suspicious at first, she became the veritable port in a storm. Passive and kindly, she recognized in him the sensitive qualities so far undetected other than by his mother.

'She used to say that I wasn't like the other boys. She called me Little Dominic after the saint, who everyone knew had a sort of feminine way about him. She seemed to look on me as a girl in a lot of ways.' It was Mother Ignatius who taught Eugene the domestic skills and he was soon a willing pupil. This comparatively happy interlude of understanding and compassion helped to ease the pain and bitterness of these unhappy years.

'At times I felt desperate. I'd see the city all lit up out there at night, and I'd hit the window and cry my eyes out. I wasn't a criminal, I hadn't done anything really wrong, so why couldn't I go free?'

If he had found a champion in the laundry, elsewhere the taunting about his sexual inclinations continued.

Still intrigued as to why he did not indulge in the usual boyish activities, the lads got up a boxing tournament and determined to conquer his spirit once and for all.

But they were disappointed. Brown 121's resilience was more of a match than they had bargained for.

'They put me up against this fellow, he was really good. I'd never boxed before in my life. I wasn't one for fights, I hated them unless I had no real choice.

'I got in there and he started taunting me: "I know what you are," he says, "you're the Devil's own, a right little poufter if ever there was one."

'That got me, I just laid into him, kicking out. It must've taken him by surprise because he ended up with an awful bleeding nose.'

The scrap resulted in 121 going on report – 'and then I got hammered again.'

Eugene began to despair, that he would never be rid of the school and his horrible existence.

'It was then that I began to hate men. I saw them for what they were and despised them. I despised myself for seeming to be one of them and this inner feeling that I was different became an absolute conviction.'

If his mother May suspected that her eldest boy was something of an odd-ball, she did not recognize it as anything more than adolescent awkwardness. Nevertheless, it was during this time at the training school that Eugene began to dress in women's clothes.

On the infrequent Sundays he was allowed a pass out, Eugene would join his family.

Together with his brother he had developed an interest in horror movies and often he would dress up, raiding his mother's wardrobe and make up bag.

'We always used to remark that he looked the image of his cousin Eileen,' says May.

'He was always done out as a female vampire, we used to laugh really and didn't think anything of it.'

Neither did Eugene at the time. He enjoyed the escapism, the theatrical gesture and the fact that he always chose to dress as a woman in preference to a man struck him only as natural.

It was such a Sunday that Eugene finally decided that enough was enough. Desperately unhappy, his thoughts in turmoil and his loathing of all men established beyond conceivable doubt, he told his parents he was home and this time he was never going back.

Fearful, but supportive to the end, the Browns packed their belongings and fled once more over the border to the sanctuary of the Republic.

3

The comparatively coddled childhood enjoyed by the little girl who was growing up across the water in Britain's industrial heartland could hardly have presented a sharper contrast.

Anne Johnson was a happy child who wanted nothing in material terms and enjoyed the security of a long established family home.

The considerable age gap between herself and the family's other three children meant that by the time she was five her sister had married and left home.

In one way this was an enormous advantage. When Anne became too much of a handful for her parents, who were already well into middle age, she went happily to her sister's, so benefiting from the love of not one household, but two. The Johnsons lived in a nondescript Birmingham suburb on a pleasant if anonymous council estate. There were not many young children in the same street, but the few there were became Anne's friends. The children in the nearby crescent were, by common consent, considered to be the enemy.

But from her toddling days Anne resisted all attempts to mould her into the female role. Dolls she was given she scornfully abandoned and an expensive new dolls' pram she gave away to a neighbour's daughter. All her girlish toys were systematically swapped for more interesting guns and battleships and she enjoyed the games of cops and robbers, cowboys and indians; indeed, her prize possession was an Indian suit and headdress, a present for her fifth birthday, and thus attired she would spend hours sitting in an old apple tree, shooting at all comers with a bow and arrows she fashioned out of garden canes. Swords were also manufactured from makeshift; and so active were her playtime pursuits that by the age of five and a half she had broken her collarbone, an arm and a bone in her foot in three separate accidents.

Eventually her parents had to face up to the fact that their daughter was a dedicated tomboy.

For her mother in particular it was a continuous disappointment that after a daughter with whom she was very close, and two robust sons, she should produce a girl who resisted all attempts to make her look and act the model of sweetness and femininity.

She would dress Anne in pretty flounced skirts, hopefully tie colourful ribbons in her tousled hair. But to no avail; Anne was at her happiest in trousers and from her first day at school would automatically rush home to change out of her tiresome school uniform and into her comfortable slacks.

The family was working class, her father skilled as a metal polisher. While he frequently changed jobs, moving from one factory to another, he was never unemployed. Mrs. Johnson busied herself looking after the family until Anne was about eight years old when she decided to supplement the family income with a part-time cleaning job.

While her mother was preoccupied with the housework, Anne would be entrusted to the care of the older children, and tagging behind, she would go exploring in the field which bordered the estate.

This magical paradise was a breeding ground for young imaginations and much of their playtime was spent in various secret dens scratched out of the scrubby undergrowths. Sometimes Anne's boy cousin, a couple of months her senior, would come to visit and join in their play. One afternoon the two five year olds ran home from the field, caught short by an urgent call of nature.

'That was the first time I began to realize something was wrong. We were both desperate to use the toilet, so Mum hurriedly opened the back door to the porch and told Peter to use the drain. Then she bundled me up to the bathroom. I remember watching Peter standing there before I was whisked off round the corner. What really hit me was how unfair it was that I couldn't use the drain too. It wasn't just because we were physically different that I got upset, but I felt I really wasn't being treated right. It was so unfair, I didn't feel like a girl, I

36

felt like Peter, so why should I be treated differently? It was all wrong.'

Such irate perception was momentary, but it set doubts into Anne's young mind which for the most part she managed to ignore – but never totally.

That her tomboyish antics were not merely transitory seemed obvious to her, if not to anyone else.

'Everyone imagined it was a phase I'd grow out of. They'd say as much amongst themselves.'

But they were wrong. Anne was simply being her natural self, and if that meant behaving like a boy, then the world would have to accept her as such. But this small girl, who was outwardly carefree, began to harbour deep and troublesome thoughts, triggered in a surprising and innocuous way.

When Anne was seven the Johnsons acquired a television set. It was the cause of much excitement and for the first week the family watched expectantly as the picture rolled relentlessly before their eyes.

'No one dared to adjust the horizontal hold to give us a proper picture. We imagined it was supposed to be like that, until someone called in and put us right.'

Anne was allowed to watch the Children's Hour in the afternoon, and it was the serialization of the folk tale, *The Prince and the Pauper* that she found thought provoking.

The story told of two boys whose deception in swopping roles was so credible that they were unable to convince their families of their plot and had to continue the falsehood for the rest of their lives.

'They had to keep quiet about who they really were, and I thought, that's me! Nobody knows the real me, I've just got to keep quiet, keep it to myself. It really upset me to realize that. As for the serial, I could only watch two episodes.'

That Anne could have confided her feelings to the family was simply out of the question. For while there was a close bond of affection between them, the family never discussed more than the mundanities of everyday life.

'We never talked about anything serious, nothing was ever mentioned about sex or anything. No one ever openly swore either. I heard Dad say "bloody" once, but nothing more.'

So while Anne recognized her own fears, she was more terrified to express them to those she loved the most.

'If I'd told them how I felt they'd have been terribly upset. My mother was a worrier at the best of times and they just wouldn't have understood. That's why I felt that all my thoughts were so dangerous. If I said anything it would've worried the people I liked the most and who I depended on. And that frightened me more than anything.'

Anne decided to push the thoughts out of her head. And with the bustle of childhood, that was not difficult; for as she bicycled furiously around and about, the conviction that life was intensely unfair would gradually recede. Most Sundays she and her father would go for a drive in one of the many cars he enjoyed tinkering with over the years. Mrs Johnson preferred to stay at home, suspicious that the vehicle would break down and leave them stranded – which it frequently did. Anne loved poking around under the bonnet with her father, laughing triumphantly when they managed to fix the temperamental engine.

Sometimes there was an obvious tension between her parents and then Anne would act as the go-between, carrying messages back and forward during the usually brief but intense disagreements. The likeliest aggravation was her father's Sunday morning drinking spree, which often became so prolonged that he missed his dinner. Mrs Johnson was not amused.

If their moods bothered Anne, she cannot recall being particularly unhappy or insecure.

'On the other hand I never went to bed ecstatically happy either. I was aware that they didn't really understand me and I always felt a barrier somewhere.'

However, Anne's sister was particularly fond of her and loved to mother her.

'In a way it was like being brought up by grandparents with my sister more like a mother to me, in terms of the generation gap.

'What it meant was I felt I had two mothers and that was a bit overpowering. I always felt the two of them presented a sort of united front to the men, and to me too. It was pretty daunting sometimes.'

At the weekend she would play with her older brothers, revelling in their masculine company and the football, wrestling and darts which were their major preoccupations; she missed them dreadfully when they were eventually called up for National Service.

As Anne reached adolescence her relatives began to recognize that her boyish stance was not going to disappear. Hair cropped short and always dressed in the inevitable trousers, Anne was frequently mistaken for a boy by those who did not know otherwise.

'Usually it happened on holiday. I loved it but my mother would tut disapprovingly and sigh as if to say "I've given up". I felt sorry for her, but I was secretly delighted.'

At eleven, Anne passed her eleven-plus examination and prepared for life at Sheldon Heath School, reputedly the second comprehensive school to open in Britain.

Anne enjoyed her schooldays, pouring much of her energy into sport. She loved soccer and had often played with her brothers, but as girls were forbidden the pitch at school, she shone at hockey instead. Her sturdy frame proved ideal for the job of goalkeeper and in time she was to play for the county team, the Warwickshire Juniors. At thirteen, her classmates were in the full throes of puberty. For Anne the thoughts and feelings pushed so firmly out of sight were to loom large as never before.

'I had one particular girlfriend, we used to hang around together. But suddenly she became interested in boys. I didn't know what to make of it. I just couldn't understand why she was reacting to them like that. It seemed and looked perfectly natural to her, but why didn't I feel that way? I couldn't fathom it out at all. I just didn't have the femininity in me to be interested.'

If she could not react like the other girls, it was equally impossible to be accepted as literally "one of the boys". She could not make friends with them in the way that she wanted, on an equal footing.

'I was labelled "girl" and they saw me as one. I was intensely jealous of them, not for their interest in girls, but for everything else. I was left in limbo.'

So while others wrangled with their first tentative involvement with the opposite sex, Anne became the confidante of one and all. A threat to no one, she kept the secrets which they could entrust to nobody else.

She soon learned the theory of growing up better than most, albeit at second hand. In practice, her only true experience of adolescence was the onset of mestruation, which Anne regarded as a loathsome and disgusting denial of her true self.

Meanwhile life at home had altered drastically. Her father, hospitalized by a serious skin disease, was not expected to live. Happily, he recovered, but returned home a changed man. No longer full of cheerful energy, he spent his spare time sitting quietly, deep in thought, rarely venturing out other than to work.

Resigning his role as head of the household, he seemed to relinquish all responsibility to his wife. For Anne the chance to confide in her parents seemed to have long gone. Once again she found self-deception the only answer.

'I tried to pretend that I was normal, that of course I was really a girl and it was silly to think or feel otherwise. It was like having an anaesthetic; I was no longer in touch with my true feelings.'

4

The Browns were on the run. Absconding from training school was a serious offence and the entire family were guilty of aiding and abetting Eugene in his escapade. For a few harrowing days they took refuge at the sea shore, managing to slip unnoticed into Dundalk, which happened to be the first town they came across after slipping over the border and following the coast road.

They had often stayed in Dundalk before on their travels and were reassured by the knowledge that friends and acquaintances would keep silent if questioned as to their whereabouts, if only as a sympathetic gesture to "poor May".

For a whole glorious fortnight Eugene savoured his illicit freedom, wandering aimlessly along the estuary to Dundalk Bay, watching the interminable waves of the Irish Sea plying their way back and forth between Ireland and the British mainland. He had few thoughts as to his future; readily accepting the philosophy maintained by his parents, indeed by most of his fellow Irish, of living solely for the moment.

It was towards the end of the two weeks that Eugene and May heard of work in Dublin and, as this city was a much greater distance from the authorities than Dundalk, the decision to move on was swiftly made.

On arriving they found a room in the usual obscure back street hotel and settled in, relieved at being able to merge anonymously into the shifting scene of city life.

But three nights later as the family slept, came a knock at the door. Eugene stumbled drowsily to answer and found himself facing Brother Stephen, an emissary from Glen Road. With him, an unfamiliar face who announced himself as a private detective, hired for the express purpose of digging out Brown 121.

The pair had spent several days on the road trailing the Browns and while clearly pleased to have run Eugene to ground, were in no mood for provocation. His frustration and anger at being discovered for once seemed too much for Eugene and he gathered up his belongings in uncharacteristic silence.

'"Never mind, 121," said Brother Stephen. "At least you can have the satisfaction of knowing you made the longest escape on record. Quite an achievement wouldn't you say?" It was ironic but I s'pose it was some consolation.'

But the hint of "bonhomie" offered small comfort for what was to come. Within half an hour Eugene was being driven at high speed north towards the border.

'It was late, almost midnight and they took me into this roadside café for something to eat. I was starving but I didn't eat a thing, I felt so choked and depressed. There seemed to be no escaping this rotten life, no matter how hard I tried.'

Nor, this time, was there to be any respite for his parents. No sooner had Eugene left than they were arrested and like their son taken directly to Belfast and into custody.

For May it was a new and terrifying experience. She was separated not only from her husband, but she had no idea where Eugene was heading and Michael, her youngest, had been swiftly whisked away into council care.

By midday after this eventful night the court had dealt with the Browns as it deemed best.

Eugene was to remain for a further nine months at the Belfast training school, with no possibility of remission. His parents were each sentenced to a month's imprisonment for their duplicity.

On the grounds of compassion for young Michael, who would have been left to fend for himself in some children's home, it was eventually agreed that May should be allowed bail. Eugene Senior was not so fortunate and duly paid his penalty.

Trapped once more within the walls of the training school, the taunting from Eugene's fellow inmates became more relentless than ever.

'They jibed me mercilessly about getting caught and that. They took great delight in giving me a pummelling whenever they got a chance. But by now I was so bitter and so used to it that to be honest it made no difference. It just made me more determined that one day I'd get back at them and at all men like them.'

At long last the penance was over, and Eugene, older and wiser now, but in a sense that the authorities would hardly have found desirable, was reunited with his family.

How to occupy himself was something of a problem. His studious avoidance of schooling left him academically fit for nothing. But at least Eugene had learnt to live by his wits.

He was a creative young man and ambitious. Dabbling in model making, using mud dug from the gardens, he created monsters and characters from the horror and science fiction movies of which he and his brother were so fond.

No one disagreed that the results were convincingly authentic. But Eugene was not content to keep his handiwork as a mere hobby; he was determined to break into the realms of theatre and television. He had little idea how to go about it, but it was what he talked and dreamed of and no one cared to disillusion him.

However, Eugene was severely handicapped; not simply because it was virtually impossible to find a way into the creative world that he aspired to, but because finding work of *any* sort in the Province was hard, let alone with no formal skills and a record of "difficult" behaviour like Eugene's.

Perhaps it was just as well that the theatricality of mask and model making and the subsequent performing gave him the excuse to dress up, usually relying as before on his mother's frugal wardrobe and cosmetics. For it was a great game and the cause of much hilarity; at the same time innocently disguising Eugene's heartfelt delight in acting openly as a woman.

It was 1969, that fateful year when Northern Ireland erupted with the troubles that continue to rage relentlessly to this day. For some time the Browns had been lodging in Belfast, in the upstairs of a two-up two-down terraced house in Dover Street.

Suddenly they found themselves in the midst of a hotbed of violence. For Dover Street ran the gauntlet between the Shankhill and the Falls roads, respective home base of the two religious factions into which centuries of hatred had finally polarized.

The Browns gave allegiance to neither side, but as they were ostensibly of Catholic persuasion, that was where their loyalties were assumed to lie. The rioting and destruction made daily life intolerable and moreover pickings were down, business bad and money scarce.

'We were literally living on the front line; I remember the day they petrol bombed the chapel. Crowds gathered and then the Specials came in, about fifteen of them in a big black van. Out they poured with their guns and simply muscled in. Just who was fighting who didn't really matter if you lived where we did. Just going outdoors and minding your own business like as not someone would take a potshot at you. Whether it was the Orange People as we called the Protestants, or your own, it was still a nightmare.'

The lawlessness led to indiscriminate attacks on the innocent. One day Eugene watched as an ambulance car, with driver and nurse, was bombed and hurtled into a neighbouring pub, killing both outright.

The sight of barricades and of tractors churning up the debris of a night's rampage was part of a pattern to which Dover Street was becoming inured.

But while the Browns witnessed the chaos of living on the front line, somehow they felt it was an unfolding scenario in which they had no part.

Until one summer's evening that is. Eugene and Michael were out with friends, Eugene Senior safer than most on one of his periodic visits to the Crumlin Road Jail.

May sat upstairs in front of the fire, for although it was July, the air was dank and chill.

She was enjoying a bite of supper, a sandwich and a cup of warming cocoa, when there was a huge explosion and she was flung to the floor.

'I didn't know where I was, there was this tremendous jolt. I managed to pick myself up and run down the stairs. Where the old lady from down below was, I had no idea. Next thing a fella was shouting "Come out, come out, you're going to be bombed".

'I needed no telling, but outside I ran straight into a man with a gun. He says to another fella, "I'm going to take this lady," and he started to pull me away. The other one says "Oh no you're not", and he grabbed me back.

'Next thing the whole house went up; seconds later and I'd have gone with it too.'

As the flames devoured the terrace, May was taken to friends, too shocked and distraught to worry about the whereabouts of her sons. It was not until noon next day that the three reunited.

'It was one of the worst nights I can remember,' says Eugene. 'We got back home to find the place on fire, nothing more than a burnt out shell. The attack was still in full flood. At one point I had to slump down in a doorway pretending to have been hit just to avoid the bullets. And all that time we had no idea where Mum was, or whether she'd been burnt alive. I was frantic.'

In the light of day the family took stock and realized they were destitute.

Every stitch of clothing, every meagre belonging, including some few sticks of furniture bought on hire purchase from Cavendish's department store, had been destroyed by the petrol bomb.

They were offered sanctuary in a local school, already in semi-permanent use as an emergency refuge.

A couple of days later they were taken out of the firing zone and housed in trailer caravans set in the comparative quiet of a predominantly Catholic area.

But May's nerves began to crack with the strain of their situation, and without visible hope of life becoming more stable they decided it was time to move on; time even to quit their beloved Ireland.

So it was that thanks to the benevolence of the Catholic church and token compensation from the Criminal Injuries Board, they found themselves on board the ferryboat bound for England, their mixed emotions at departing the homeland blurred by violent seasickness.

'I was the only one not throwing up,' recalls Eugene. 'It was pretty rough, but at least I felt optimistic about starting over somewhere fresh.'

Once again, the results were to fall somewhat short of his expectations.

The Browns' new home was to be a one-room bedsit in

London's Paddington. The rent was ten pounds a week, the bathroom shared with the landlord – one Jimmy Bull and his family.

It did not take long for May to unpack the two suitcases of bare necessities they had acquired with the compensation; nor for Eugene Senior and his eldest to discover that finding work in the metropolis was no easier than it was in Belfast. Nor did the prospects improve as the days grew into weeks and their only source of income was the State.

'We were back on the breadline and with nothing to do all day, no friends to meet up with, it was very depressing.'

Realizing their problems, Jimmy Bull offered Eugene casual work on his icecream round. Eugene was reluctant at first; his brushes with the law had left him anxious to stay out of trouble, and with no cards or tax arrangements he feared being picked up by the police.

But Jimmy was desperate; the tourist season was in full fling and he needed all the help he could get.

Eugene gave in and for a brief but busy time was to be found plying "super whips" and choc ices in London's most popular spots, in particular Hyde Park and down Petticoat Lane.

'It was something of a rip-off really. We charged the foreigners forty pence for a cone, which was a lot of money then.'

One especially fraught Sunday morning Eugene was manning the van alone when two policemen strolling by appeared to be watching him with particular interest.

In retrospect Eugene realized he was being unnecessarily sensitive.

'But it was enough. I was convinced they were on to me so I packed up as fast as possible and fled. That was the end of my venture into icecream.'

What with one thing and another, life in England was a disappointment. It was peaceful enough to allow May's nerves to recover and so it was by mutual decision that they booked their passage back to Ireland.

'We weren't exactly looking forward to it. The violence terrified me. But we didn't seem to have much choice; at least in Belfast we had some contacts and there was a chance of scratching a living somehow.'

It was winter and with the Dover Street house written off,

46

the Browns were offered an apartment in the Catholic stronghold of Ballamurphy. If anything the political situation had worsened during their brief sojourn. The tower blocks stood watch over the battling streets and while the two communities maintained a relentless harangue, there was a common new target, the British Army.

Ironically the peace-keeping force had become the focal point of everyone's hatred and tormenting the soldiers a daily pastime.

For Eugene the hostilities only served to heighten his growing depression. Life seemed pointless and he began to despair of ever finding a job or a true role in life.

But the biggest burden was the inner disturbance that arose from his firm belief that he was trapped in the wrong body. Everything was a sham – and as he reached adulthood the certainty of his true sexuality became a major preoccupation.

'I had felt trapped inside my maleness for so long that the resentment was spilling out. I found myself suffering from terrible black moods which made me unbearable to live with. There was no outlet, no freedom to express myself. Ballamurphy was hardly the place for such a revelation, so I had to suppress it.'

To do so, Eugene found himself going to intolerable lengths. But if in doing so he hoped to find peace of mind then he was mistaken.

'I tried to convince myself that the only way to get by was to try and conform to what everyone expected of me as a normal, healthy heterosexual male.'

As far as the Irish community was concerned that meant two things: he had to join the all-male drinking school and find himself a girlfriend.

To Eugene both were anathema. He was never a great drinker and, despising as he did most men, the thought of having to share their exclusive company was something he could barely begin to make sense of. Nonetheless, he made one or two token attempts to join in, propping up the bar along with the best of them.

'I hated their men talk. They were forever putting women down, deriding them, making the usual dirty jokes at their expense. It got at me inside, I found it vulgar, as if it was me they were getting at.'

To add to his unease the burly Irish Catholics took obvious

delight in taunting Eugene, whom they could simply not figure out.

'They thought I was queer, no doubt about that. When they'd had a few they'd give me hell, poking and nudging me and making snide insinuations.'

Indeed homosexual relationships were readily on offer; and when Eugene gave them a vehement rebuff, their confusion was complete.

'"What are you then if you're not a poufftah?" they'd say. How could I tell them the truth? There wasn't a hope in hell that they'd understand.'

Unable to form sound friendships with the men, Eugene found himself growing more and more lonely.

Michael was his one real friend, but he was only a boy. The two men he did get on with reasonably well joined the IRA, there was no way Eugene wanted to get politically involved and therefore grew distant from them.

Conversely, women found Eugene good company. They talked with him easily and would trust him with their most intimate thoughts.

'It was odd really, but they'd tell me all about their boyfriends, their sex lives, their period pains, everything. What exactly they saw me as I wasn't sure. But they were good mates and seemed to feel that they could lean on me as they couldn't with the other men.'

Before the Browns had been long in Ballamurphy one such young lady, named Sally, made it clear that her intent was not merely platonic.

For Eugene then, came a fresh complication and one which until now he had purposefully avoided.

'My sole encounters with girls had amounted to a trip to the ice rink and once or twice to the pictures, all completely innocent, I'd simply wanted someone to go with.'

But what Sally was suggesting was a different proposition. 'She wanted me as a proper boyfriend, she found me attractive physically and she wanted me to sleep with her.'

Eugene was thrown into a panic. He liked Sally right enough, but how could he make love to any woman when he felt himself to be female?

'I wasn't even sure that my body would function normally as a male, I didn't want to feel close to a woman in that way.'

48

But Sally persisted and the social pressures Eugene was under were becoming more oppressive.

So he took Sally to bed.

'Or rather she took me. I don't know what I expected but it was the strangest feeling, as though it wasn't really me lying there at all, but someone else doing it.

'My overwhelming thought was that it wasn't right. I wanted to be the woman, I wanted someone to make love to me. I didn't know what Sally was feeling, I didn't ask her much. In terms of fulfilment I felt nothing, I just wanted to get it over and done with.'

By losing his virginity, Eugene succeeded in his sham and, for the time being, his sexuality was no longer a topic of endless speculation. Now he too could boast of his exploits in the pub.

The deception was reinforced when he took up with Mary, a student nurse. They met through her brother and Eugene would spend much of his time at their home near the flats.

The Protestant district was only five streets away and going out, even to the cinema, was a major operation which involved avoiding the armoured car patrols. In Mary, Eugene found a willing and sympathetic listener, and they spent many hours alone together, rather than going out.

When they eventually made love the inner turmoil finally spilled out as Eugene told Mary his burdensome secret.

'I can't tell you what a relief it was to share it with someone. She seemed to understand, but of course it made it impossible for her to look on me as a boyfriend.'

Eugene's sexual encounters had not helped much in his pursuit of personal happiness.

'I s'pose I'd hoped that by trying to act normally I'd not only convince everyone else, but I'd find out that that was how I really wanted to be and that after all I was no different to other men. It didn't. It just helped to confirm what I already knew; that I was a woman.'

While Eugene fought to reconcile himself, May once again fell sudden victim of the violence.

Cooking supper one evening a bullet winged through the kitchen door, missing her by a short inch.

After this incident, the Browns decided that they could no longer live in trouble-torn Ulster, for them it was no longer worthy of being called home. So, sickened and disenchanted they packed their bags yet again, and left, this time forever.

5

Anne Johnson may have been growing up as Eugene's contemporary, but there all similarity of lifestyle ended. While the young Irishman drifted in a kind of adolescent abyss, Anne was proving to have an above average intelligence and to be ambitious. Anaesthetized against her innermost thoughts she poured her youthful energy into her schoolwork, doing well at O-level exams and surprising her parents by wanting to stay on for the sixth-form with the eventual aim of a university place.

The other Johnson children had all left school at sixteen, ready for work and to make their contribution to the house-keeping. Indeed no other child in the road had as yet ever contemplated higher education, let alone university. While the Johnsons were proud of their daughter's ability and gave her every support, they were nevertheless puzzled by her chosen path.

'I admit I wasn't an easy child to bring up, I must've seemed contrary from the start. I wanted us to be close and for them to understand me, but I'd long discovered I couldn't talk to them about things so I decided to go my own way. I couldn't really understand their line of thinking any more than they could fathom me out.'

Not that her parents were anything but supportive once her mind was made up. But at least they took comfort in one sign of apparent normality.

At sixteen Anne found herself a boyfriend.

Among her classmates was Andrew Biddulph, an amenable young fellow who was studying hard to live up to his teachers' expectations as a potential scientist. Chemistry was his subject and he was working with intense enthusiasm to get to university.

To Anne, Andrew was at first a great friend, later a romantic distraction.

From the first, theirs was a relationship built on drifting sand and circumstance, a cosy amiability that was to lead far beyond its original promise and purpose.

'I wanted to seem normal, to prove to myself that I was like all the other girls.

'Andrew and I got on well together, we understood each other, we had the same ideas about life, we'd talk about things and it took off from there.

'He was the first member of the opposite sex I'd really got along with and felt at home with. He saw me as a girl of course; if I saw him as a boyfriend it was as a friend first, a boy second.'

Still, to all outward intents and purposes a boyfriend he was, and for Anne that was a welcome relief. She could now convince the world – and to some degree herself – that she was a normal heterosexual female. After a childhood of perplexity and self-questioning, she was able to play out the accepted girlish role with some equanimity.

Eventually the A-level examinations loomed large and Andrew and Anne began to contemplate the future. Anne was hoping for a place at the University of Surrey to study Human Relations, and it seemed natural at the time that Andrew should do likewise. However, Anne failed one vital Biology exam and was suddenly faced with being left behind to repeat the year, or, taking second best, a teacher training place at college in the north of England.

She could face neither, and determined as ever to have her own way despite this setback, she managed to get herself onto a business studies course at the City of London College. It meant two years' studying before she could eventually get onto a full degree course, hopefully alongside Andrew, who had won through to Surrey.

So the two eighteen-year-olds left home for London. It was the middle of the "swinging sixties", a time of changing morality and exciting new freedoms such as had never been witnessed before. While Anne's family were naturally unhappy to see her depart for the capital with boyfriend in tow, they were confused as to what stance they should or indeed could take, without incurring the wrath of two youngsters caught up in the new permissive society. Still, they were also secretly relieved that Anne was not facing London alone.

They need not have worried. The pair had no thought of overstepping the mark and upsetting their families. So while they were eager to share their new independence as much as possible, it never occurred to them to live together, not yet anyway.

Andrew settled into the university hall of residence in Battersea, south of the Thames, while Anne found herself several miles away, north of the river, in the Jewish quarter of suburban Stamford Hill.

Her first taste of living in digs was to prove more of an experience than she had bargained for. Her landlady was an elderly Jewish matron who was bordering on senility; her sole companion her son, a bachelor in his forties. The pair were devoted.

The domestic situation seemed amicable enough. Anne had her own room but could use the kitchen to do her own cooking. Each morning she would catch the bus to college, meeting up with Andrew at weekends and sometimes once or twice during the week too.

But another man was finding this young lady, fresh from school, an attraction, and that was the landlady's son. Before long his sexual advances became a major part of any conversation he attempted to hold with Anne as she busied herself in the kitchen. His hints were embarrassingly frank, his pictorial library of dirty books a feeble outlet for his tremendous frustrations.

'He was simply sex crazy. For the most part I managed to fend him off by ignoring the innuendos. I might've been young but I think I was fairly level headed.'

Eventually her admirer could stand the rebuff no longer and appeared in her room with pants round his ankles, brandishing his circumcised penis.

'Take a good look, this one's Jewish,' he said. Unabashed by such affrontery, Anne dissolved into laughter. After that all problems ceased and life returned to comparative normality. There were other diversions to which Anne was prepared to give wholeheartedly of her time, not least of which was the

53

Young Socialist movement. It was within this political group allied at this time to the Young Trotskyists, that Anne and Andrew began to make friends; they would spend long hours mulling over the doctrines and dogmas of the respective parliamentary parties. But it was not all simply harmless badinage. Their commitment to a true democracy was genuine enough and is one Anne has maintained.

'To me, with my personal dilemma, what mattered most was that we should have a free world where men and women were offered a definite choice in life and where everyone was regarded as equal. If that sounds totally idealistic it was the only way I could see my ever being allowed to choose my sexual role. And that was worth fighting for.'

Ironically as Anne threw herself wholeheartedly into being a student activist to achieve that freer society, she was using it partly as a diversion to firmly repress her own sense of imbalance.

'I still wouldn't admit to myself that I was play acting, that this wasn't reality at all. I kept on tramping on my true self, on my masculinity.'

Her relationship with her fellow students was superficially like that of any other strident and articulate young female going through college at the time. She did not have a lot of friends, but a lot of acquaintances made through Andrew and the debating society. Their main circle were committed socialists and when, after a year at college, Anne managed to work her way into the university, even though she left her course incomplete, it was within the political faction that the pair began to shine.

In a short while Anne became the secretary and though it meant a lot of hard work she was as much motivated by the ideals of the cause as she was exhilarated by the job of organizing her fellow students.

'I was beginning to love London, to enjoy the power I had to motivate the others,'

Student unrest was often all-too evident on the streets of the capital. Most weekends saw a demonstration or protest march, although some cynically dubbed this new mood of radicalism a "sparetime occupation."

To some extent that was true. To the radicals among these children of the sixties Bob Dylan's maxim that "the times, they

54

are a-changing" became a byword. So it was with Surrey's young socialists, and Andrew and Anne were among the leaders at every anti-nuclear, anti-Vietnam rally, factory strike or march with which they felt an affinity.

'It was exciting, we thrived on it. Andrew could be very forthright at meetings and if people thought we were a bit odd-ball they agreed that because of that we were well-suited.'

Anne had never outgrown her attachment to jeans and trousers and she wore them continuously. But she was not unattractive, with long flowing hair and a friendly willingness to listen, which intrigued quite a few of the male students.

But this initial welcome soon froze when any tried to chat her up.

'I was really horrible to them, I'd give them an icy stare and cut them dead. It was very effective, but they came to the conclusion that I was very strange. Little did they know!'

Her brush-off technique, plus her unfeminine choice of clothes earned Anne the tag of being something of a feminist.

"Women's Lib" was still very much in its infancy, but because of her apparent independence, even from Andrew, and her open-minded ideals, her contemporaries regarded her as a free spirit.

Which is why her next and most outrageous decision had them completely foiled.

Anne announced that she was going to marry Andrew.

In retrospect, and with the knowledge of Anne's conviction that she was trapped in the wrong gender, it is difficult to understand why she made such a drastic decision.

At the time, it all seemed much simpler. She and Andrew had been together since they were both sixteen; it was expected and welcomed at home that one day they would wed; and as they both faced the new academic year, Anne's second at the university, with nowhere to live, it made sense to get together.

But conformity still held a niggling importance and while it would have been simpler to live openly in sin, there were the folks back home to consider. Andrew respected his family, while Anne still confessed to being frightened of hers. Twelve years later, Andrew recalls their reasoning:

'We'd been together since the sixth-form at school, through college, and getting married, well, it was a very cushy and easy way of doing things.

'It seemed a natural progression somehow, almost a question of well, why not?'

Any reasons why indeed they should not, Anne kept firmly locked away inside herself.

'All my university friends must've thought I was mad because, in one sense, I was probably the most liberated lady there. To want to conform, to tie myself down to one man like that must have seemed a total contradiction of all we'd been fighting for. And I suppose they were right. It was a contradiction but not in the way they saw it.'

And so that summer vacation Anne and Andrew said goodbye to their friends and went home to Birmingham.

The Johnsons took the news with mixed feelings. They liked Andrew well enough and were pleased that he intended to do the decent thing by Anne. They would have preferred it if they had waited awhile, until they had finished their studies, but generously they gave the couple their blessing. Anne celebrated her twentieth birthday in July and they set the date for a Saturday in September.

Both had long since rejected religion and were adamant that the wedding should not be in church.

But Mrs Johnson was deluding herself in hoping that she and her daughter could at last share the female preoccupation of shopping for outfits and a trousseau. No amount of cajoling could persuade Anne to make even modest wedding plans and right up to twenty-four hours before the ceremony, her poor distraught mother had visions of Anne reciting her marriage lines in her jeans.

'She kept on nagging at me to go out and buy something. Eventually at about four o'clock on the Friday afternoon I went into town and literally bought the first thing I saw.'

So Anne the bride turned up at the register office in a fashionable white mini-dress.

'It was so short I must've looked as though I was off to play tennis. It had a scarf round the neck and I su'pose it was really very nice. To me it was a token gesture. I felt very uncomfortable and conspicuous.'

If Anne imagined she looked incongruous it was typical of how she felt about the whole affair.

'The only way I could have let things get this far was by treating the whole situation like a play. All the way through I felt I was on the outside watching it all happening to someone else. I felt very alone and very afraid. I stood there looking at our relatives and at Andrew and repeating the words, but all the time the man inside me was saying "You stupid fool. What a mess you've got yourself into.'"

So twenty years of living as a female was effectively consummated as Anne took just twenty minutes to become Mrs Andrew Biddulph.

6

Anne and Andrew had enjoyed a sexual relationship for some time, so in terms of intimacy their marriage made little difference. If anyone had queried whether they were in love their answer would have been "yes", based on an affectionate companionship, a sharing of ideals. Theirs was a genuine affection and Andrew at least took their union seriously.

'While it seemed a natural progression that we should marry, for me our relationship was permanent and that was it, as I thought, for life.'

Anne's hankering for stability against her inner turmoil meant that she too was prepared to play at being a wife with some genuine intentions to see the marriage work. It was only years later, the divorce pending, that Andrew read some of Anne's diaries of that time.

Days before her wedding Anne had written: "He'll do, until someone better comes along."

'I never guessed she felt that way.' Nor did he guess at his wife's terrifying secret.

'We liked each other very much, we were still the best of friends and all that added up to what seemed a compatible relationship.'

Indeed, for Anne this was a time of respite from her inward isolation. She could now concentrate her energies on being a married woman and draw strength from the social prestige and security of having a partner.

'Sex between us was passionate in those early days. If that sounds a contradiction, then in retrospect I can only say I was like a young boy venturing on a relationship of childlike homosexuality; and that was a strong physical need.'

The wedding over, the Biddulphs returned to university and prepared to set up home. Andrew's unconventional approach to most things in life at that time was, for Anne, one of his main attractions. When he suggested that they buy a boat to live on she was intrigued. The idea also seemed a practical one, being a comparatively cheap form of accommodation considering the high price most Londoners pay for a roof over their heads.

After much searching they found an old canal barge moored on the outskirts of Birmingham. It set them back all of fifty pounds, and while sadly neglected, the addition of a 1928 Morris Navigator engine made it a reasonable proposition. Once the engine had been installed, the newly-weds loaded their belongings aboard and prepared to chug the hundred or so miles down the canal to London.

Romantic notions of boat life were shortlived. After ten miles the engine seized. There was nothing they could do but to manually pull their new house down the canal. It was a tortuous trip and a disastrous start to married life, let alone the new academic year.

But the spirit of adventure prevailed and eventually the exhausted couple reached London, spending their last few pence on the luxury of a tow out of the canal system and up the River Thames. Then, they meandered to the River Wey, a less significant and quieter mainstream.

By this time half of the university term had passed with the couple preoccupied in sorting out moorings. Weybridge seemed a good enough place for the moment, but it was a fair commuting distance from the comparative solitude of their Surrey riverbank to the university campus at Guildford.

As winter approached, their floating love-nest seemed to survive the elements, despite its outward resemblance to a badly battered coal barge.

Inside they were snug enough, the only major drawback being at the back of the boat where it tended to take in water.

'Our first real, tremendous rows were over the baling out. It needed doing every morning which was a real chore. Once I got so fed up I remember stomping off for a couple of hours on my own.'

Every spare moment was spent trying to find better moorings, which proved difficult. When the strain of life afloat plus the constant journeying to and fro became too much, they would stay overnight at the university, sharing a friend's room.

If it wasn't all marital bliss and cosy domesticity, the two twenty-year-olds were thoroughly enjoying their bohemian lifestyle. Like students universally they were permanently broke, but their status both as a married couple and as boat people gave them a certain prestige in campus circles.

By Christmas the boat had behaved itself and stopped leaking for some three weeks, so they reckoned it was safe to go home to their families. It was a happy holiday for the Johnsons, pleased as they were to indulge their daughter and her new husband whom they had not seen since the wedding. Anne apparently suited married life, as did Andrew. Their fears for Anne began to recede; at long last it looked as though she was turning out to be normal.

If all seemed momentarily harmonious, the end of the vacation brought an unexpected setback; the pair returned to find their home virtually sunk, only a slender chain tethered to a tree preventing it from total immersion.

With enormous effort the barge was salvaged, but all their possessions were saturated, Anne's essays completed for assessment, ruined.

After several trips to the local laundrette to rejuvenate their clothes and bedding and with the help of air driers from a nearby factory to dry out the sodden bed mattress, the Biddulphs abandoned ship and fell on the mercy of the university who loaned them a room.

Such was the pattern of that first year of married life. In spring they hired a tug to pull them back up the Thames and through the Grand Union Canal. It proved to be quite a journey, the tug setting such a pace that the beading on the corking layer of the barge was pulled adrift and had to be plugged up with paper as they went.

Their new pitch was near Southall, so making the daily journey to lectures even more arduous. But they were back on the canal, which almost made the feeling of permanent "jetlag" from commuting worthwhile.

This point in their life was certainly eventful. A week before Easter, they had burglars; two lads who had been lurking around took Anne's knife and a cigarette lighter. They were subsequently caught and, giving it little more thought, Anne and Andrew made their usual holiday visit to Birmingham –

only to find the boat smashed to kindling on their return.

'We felt completely sick. Everything was floating in the cut, it was hopeless. I ran along the towpath chasing a dustbin lid that was floating away. It was fruitless to bother, but I was so angry I had to do something.'

Whether the mindless vandalism was a work of retribution by the two thieves could never be proven, though the Biddulphs had their suspicions.

Whoever the culprits, it was the end of the couple's days on the canal. Totally depressed, they went back home and with the help of the Johnsons, managed to salvage odd bits and pieces which they towed to the Midlands and piled onto a trailer.

Despite the unorthodox domestic upheaval, interspersed with a busy programme of student political activity, they both somehow managed to pass their end of year exams.

The summer was spent supplementing their grants with holiday jobs, Andrew labouring on assorted building sites, Anne joining other women on the line at a cake factory.

Commonsense prevailed that second autumn, and they abandoned all whimsical ideas of finding another boat. Instead they took lodgings right in Guildford within walking distance of the campus. It was no recompense for the outdoor life.

'We'd come to love the countryside and the people we met on the barges. Now we felt closed in. We'd lost our first home and that left a deep emptiness. For a long time I felt very upset and I had this tremendous hankering to get back on the water.'

Life became a mundane slog as Andrew prepared for his finals. Anne too became absorbed in her studies. While she found the human and physical sciences (involving chemistry, mathematics and some complex crystallography) difficult and not the course she had ideally wanted to take, what she lacked in ability she made up for in enthusiasm.

The following summer they spent with the Johnsons while Andrew waited for his results. Their future had never really been discussed, Anne assuming that they would both graduate and follow their respective careers. But her delight at Andrew getting a passable degree was to be sharply curtailed. No sooner was the result out than Andrew announced he had found a job as an industrial chemist, in his home town.

Anne was dumbfounded. She still had a year to complete at

Guildford and here was her husband coolly deciding to stay in the Midlands, a hundred miles north.

'Thinking about it later I realized he hadn't tried very hard to get a job in the south and that this was what he'd envisaged all along. It was the first time he'd kept his plans from me, I didn't seem to count.'

And when it came to choosing between giving up University and keeping the marriage together or going back alone:

'He knew damn well what I'd decide, although at the time I didn't imagine he could read me so well.'

For Anne there was no real choice.

Despite her apparent independence and liberated stance, she could not face returning to student life alone, with the risk that all her innermost feelings would once again come to the surface.

'I was using my marriage as an insurance policy against everything I felt and knew myself to be deep within. If I gave up that outer respectability and security then I would be laying myself open to misinterpretation: because of the way I looked people were inclined to think of me as a liberated lesbian until they knew I was married.

'My feelings had to be kept down and having a husband made it all the more easier. I had to give up and stick with him.'

For Andrew his reasoning held no such depths.

'I needed a job, I was offered one that sounded good and I took it. Anne would most likely have failed her degree anyway to be honest – she found it tough going – and I didn't reckon she was that bothered.'

Anne disagreed and felt a resentment at his apparent chauvinism, a feeling that was to grow in the coming months.

So it was after the unconventional freedom they had become used to, they found themselves moving in with the Johnsons while they saved for a house of their own.

It was a period that could have proved stultifying. But for Anne it turned out to be a welcome respite.

'Again in retrospect, I was very much the little boy, glad to cling to the security of home. My emotions seemed frozen in time and if things were in a turmoil, then to retreat into the bosom of my family, like a young adolescent, was a reassurance. For a while I could stop being Mrs Biddulph, the married lady.'

Andrew was grateful for his in-laws' support. He got on well with them, enjoying the loving care lavished on them both by Mrs Johnson, a care he had never known from his young wife.

It was as if Anne had never left home. 'I didn't have to do a thing, cook a meal, do the washing. Mum did it all, and I must admit I was glad to let her.'

While Anne plodded away as a clerk with the World Bureau of Statistics – 'It sounded good but it was a dead end job' – their building society account grew steadily until they had enough for a substantial deposit. A year had passed and the radicalism of their student days seemed to be deserting Andrew. Anne remained fiery.

'When it came to finding a house I began to realize just how much he wanted to settle down and live an ordinary married life. It was as if we were gradually drifting apart in our ideas of what this marriage should be all about.'

The arguments began when Andrew set his heart on a coachman's cottage, set incongruously in the smart executive belt of Solihull, an area much favoured by the industrial belt's bourgeoisie.

Anne's socialist principles were offended at the thought of living amongst the *nouveau riche*. Her sensibilities told her that by making this commitment to a life as a suburban housewife she would be more stifled and trapped by the sham she had become than she was by the knowledge of her true sexual identity.

Andrew elated, Anne tortured with enormous misgivings, they moved in.

7

The Browns' return to England coincided with the arrival of Bruce Lee fever. This celluloid phenomenon with his daring exploits in the martial art of Kung Fu gripped the imagination of a generation hungry for an outlet for their youthful aggressions. Not for them the reality of the Belfast street battles. Instead, thanks to Lee, the martial arts craze was in full flood and it swept Eugene and his young brother along with the best of them. Eugene had already dabbled in these martial arts to the extent of taking lessons in Belfast. Now the full commercial blitz of the Kung Fu school fired his imagination as never before and he became hooked.

It was easy to find others to share his enthusiasm in their cosmopolitan London neighbourhood. But Eugene soon tired of messing about with the lads in the backyard, in improvised and poor imitation of their hero. He wanted to know more, to study the martial arts seriously.

Inevitably still out of work, he would spend his days wandering aimlessly through the Chinese quarter in London's Soho, browsing for hours among the bookshops of Gerrard Street, absorbing all he could from the numerous bizarre volumes and colourful magazines. He became a familiar figure to the Chinese booksellers, for few Europeans ventured so regularly into their domain. Despite his poor schooling, Eugene set about improving his knowledge of self defence from this motley selection of imported eastern manuals.

'I couldn't understand a word of the text although I used to love looking at the shape of the language. But I realized this was the pure Kung Fu, Wing Chung, unlike Bruce Lee's style it was uncorrupted by western influence, and that's what I found fascinating.'

By painstakingly following the photographs and diagrams, Eugene would copy a movement as much as three hundred times a day until he got it right.

Before long his preoccupation became an obsession which his family found difficult to comprehend.

'He'd practise and practise all these weird movements over and over, dead serious he was,' says May. 'Drove us all mad with it he did, and young Michael, he got him interested in it too.'

The brothers both had naturally wiry builds ideal for the defensive arts and before long they became friendly with the Lungs, a Chinese Malaysian family, themselves Kung Fu experts.

Intrigued by Eugene's sober dedication, they gradually revealed to him their personal knowledge of the ancient art. From them the Browns were to learn movements and techniques scarcely known in Britain, nor indeed for that matter, outside China. In return for such exclusive teaching, the Lungs demanded strict discipline and training.

So determined was he to attain the supreme physical fitness that marked the true exponent that Eugene began a daunting daily exercise routine. It began with a lengthy run in Hyde Park, followed by large doses of skipping, jumping and general stamina training.

'The more I pushed myself the better I felt and the more determined I became to get better and better. It was all I could think about, all I cared about.'

Therein lay the clue to Eugene's sudden and complete obsession.

The humiliation of those years at training school, the incongruity of his physical appearance with his inner femininity, and the dismal failure to match up to a normal manhood had left him with very little left to live for.

'My nerves were about to crack up and I desperately needed something to cling on to.'

That something, being the first to come along, was Kung Fu. Fortunately it fitted the bill nicely.

The sense of culture, the physical identity with a mystical past that was imperturbably woven through the art, struck deep with this highly confused character. That it also appealed to his sense of dramatic artistry and showmanship was a bonus. In all it offered him an escape route, a chance to develop beyond the bounds of plain, crazy Eugene Brown, into a supremo who was to be admired rather than scorned; and above everything else it afforded him the ideal chance to score physically over the male he hated so much.

Such motivations could only lead to success and within a matter of months Eugene was proving himself to have a real aptitude. Michael, keen to follow his big brother, became a quick and able partner.

It was physically punishing but the bumps and bruises incurred during practice only hardened Eugene's resolve. Gradually his fanaticism, for he admits that is what it had become, took full hold of his vivid imagination.

More than ever he strove to deny his Irish birthright and to reject his body which filled him with such disgust.

As he became more acceptable to the Chinese so his understanding of their culture grew, to the extent that he began to identify personally with the East.

'I was always very courteous to them, I let them take the lead and watched how they acted towards one another, and did likewise. I saw that being white it was unlikely they'd teach me everything they knew, but what I did learn from them was good.'

He watched privately the skills they did not care to show in public, movements carried out with tremendous presence and performed at a surprisingly slow but graceful pace.

As he blended further into this closed society, so he learnt the steps of the Dragon and Lion dances, so popular at Chinese New Year.

But these were peripheral to what was to follow.

He began to embrace the Orient in every way, preferring the Chinese to his English friends, and even adopting the name of Lung or the Dragon, in deference to the father of his Chinese teachers.

So it was that Eugene Brown, the rebellious traveller child from Ulster, became Eugene Lung, a mystical master of Kung Fu who preferred not to reveal exactly where or how he had been born. By now the self-deception had become a reality. No one doubted his physical skills, but what mattered more to Eugene was the spiritual, meditative power which only came with rigorous and continuous study.

His ultimate goal was to achieve the Chi Kung, the internal

power that would enable him to mentally outgrow his human form and the lie it symbolized.

To do so he delved deeper into the origins of Kung Fu, to the ten basic exercises contrived by Buddha and the version as learnt by the Tibetan monks from the Lamas, the White Crane.

It was this form that Eugene felt most akin to, the sweeping, graceful sets dance-like in their mimicry of the great white bird. This, plus the meditation, gave him a strength which later enabled him to perform feats that the layman found incredible.

'I was working harder than I had ever done in my life. But the compensation was that at least I was staying sane, keeping my nerves on an even keel. It was a great discipline, it helped me to lock my problems and feelings away, to push them out for long periods of time.'

But whenever Eugene saw the Chinese women perform, he felt an agonizing pain deep inside.

'They had a certain hardness, a coolness which I found tantalizing. But the yearning inside me was unbearable. I knew I was good, but I wanted to be like them, for the world to watch me perform not in this shape, but as a woman.'

It was yet one more predictable irony that the men imagined his interest was plain voyeurism.

Eugene's appetite for knowledge of the orient was now insatiable, and it was Hong Kong that strangely disturbed him most. He sat through every available film that featured the colony in whatever detail, especially those involving the martial arts. He astounded the Chinese who originated from there with his vivid descriptions of roads and buildings, his knowledge of the smallest districts. How he came to know all this remains inexplicable.

'I'd listened a lot, read a lot, seen the films and photographs, but it wasn't just that − it was as if the old sixth sense, the visionary power I'd had as a child had come back to me in force. I wasn't trying to kid anyone, I'd just find myself coming out with information that even I didn't know I knew!'

Stretched taut by the physical and mental rigours that he demanded of himself, Eugene was now taking himself very seriously.

He went along to karate and Kung Fu classes to observe and to pass judgement.

'I saw the way they were teaching and it was nothing like

what I had learnt from the Chinese. Everyone seemed to be cashing in on the commercialism, and I realized I knew more than most of the men who were calling themselves teachers.'

He began to appreciate that he too could turn his new found skill to advantage. The Browns' impecunious state had not improved and as before, work was non-existent. The grass seemed greener elsewhere and so it was decided to move north to Birmingham, being the nearest large city to offer prospects and the sanctuary of an Irish community.

By Brown standards, it was a comparatively good move; their fellow Irish welcomed them to their inner city stronghold in the downtown district of Aston, to the bedsit Victorian terraces of Trinity Road. Here they were to stay for several months, Eugene senior building up a fairly successful business as a gardener, while his son continued his preoccupation with the Kung Fu.

But conditions were cramped and when they were offered better rooms in neighbouring Handsworth they decided to move. Handsworth sported a multiracial population and a large and pleasant park. It was here that Eugene continued his daily fitness programme and with Michael practised his White Crane and the more spectacular Wu Su acrobatics.

They soon acquired a regular and fascinated audience of young blacks who were themselves crazy about Kung Fu.

Flattered by their attentions, the Browns would give their most flamboyant demonstrations. Eugene in particular loved showing off, by now he was a self-confessed exhibitionist. It followed that their audience clamoured for him to teach them his "tricks".

'I was reluctant because they just didn't understand that it could be lethal. But eventually we got friendly with a few of them and I agreed to teach them in our back garden.

'I had one rule – never kick, except for your own exercise and definitely no weapons, or I'd threaten never to teach them again.'

The majority of his pupils were not dissuaded by his tough discipline and soon Eugene had a small and flourishing little business going. Unable to find proper employment he realized he could use his martial arts to advantage.

'I needed to buy equipment, weapons and such, and so I started charging for private tuition. It was really the first time

I'd ever earned a living and what was even better was that I was making money out of something I enjoyed.'

Totally preoccupied now, Eugene found himself with little time for introspection regarding his sexual ambiguity. But fate had taken him in hand; by acquiring a taste for teaching, Eugene was set on a path that was to radically change his life, indeed his very being.

8

Eugene's escapism was for the moment serving him well, but Anne's misgivings about her current lifestyle were proving sadly true.

She was angry at her husband's determination to buy the cottage and her annoyance did not die down once they had settled in. For the cornerstone of their relationship to date had been sharing, from ideals down to the daily chores.

Now suddenly not only had the decision of where to live been of his choosing, but he also began to renege on other things, not least the housework.

'We'd always taken it in turns, both working, but he suddenly asserted his maleness and began leaving it all to me.'

Anne's reaction was one of jealous hurt. Perhaps for the first time in her life she was not having things all her own way.

More importantly, she hated playing the housewife, indeed she had no idea of how to be one or any desire to learn. For Andrew to begin treating her as "the little woman" was nothing short of an insult. To add injury to this smarting insult, she was envious of him being able to vaunt his male arrogance so naturally and openly.

Anne was infuriated and confused by this turnabout.

'I had this feeling of dread when it came to looking after the house, doing the washing, and it really grieved me to see him out there enjoying himself while I was stuck inside. I remember one day I was doing the washing up and I felt so angry I started to cry.'

The resentment which began when she had to abandon her studies was determined to grow.

The Biddulphs were regarded as somewhat of an odd couple

71

by their neighbours. One enjoyment the couple shared was tinkering with old cars and there was always a motley collection of bangers in various states of disarray cluttering the front drive. Andrew was in his element: 'But we must have stuck out like a sore thumb, it always looked a shambles. We usually had about three cars on the go and if one broke down I'd use another.'

To Anne this was a fascination she had held since those childhood outings with her father. Andrew taught her the basic skills of mechanics and together they spent six months hotting up an ancient Mini for her. 'It had an additional nine brake horsepower over a standard engine and used to take off like a rocket.'

No sooner had they finished that than Anne started hankering after a sports car.

'That's how she was, plain obstinate, always burning to go one better. She wanted to put us in debt for it too. I told her she could have one when we'd got some money in the bank.'

Such trivial disagreements, part and parcel of most marriages, seemed to magnify in Anne's eyes, sensitive as she was to any threat to her self-assertion, her independence.

Still, there was the consolation of work. Andrew had moved on from his original job and was now a quality controller at the giant British Leyland car works. 'You would reject parts only to find them coming back to you.' After a spell of working on a building site, he decided to fall back on teaching. He found a post in maths and general science: 'But I must admit it was a bit of a let down.'

Anne meanwhile had gone into the social services as a welfare assistant. At last she had found something to interest her intellectually and while she kept her personal dilemma a close secret, it unconsciously helped her understand some of her clients' problems.

But while she was careful not to let it interfere with her work, in her private life her sexual ambivalence began to play havoc.

'I suddenly found myself physically and emotionally attracted to other women. It had never happened before, but it became irresistible, a feeling that grew in spite of myself.'

It began innocently enough with a colleague.

'We used to meet in the corridor and look away from each

72

other. We smoked the same brand of cigarettes and she would often come to cadge one off me. It was amazing, we would find ourselves shaking when we talked to one another.'

Such heady excitement was a new experience for Anne. She had never felt aroused in this fashion by a man and yet how could she react so to another woman? Even more incomprehensible to her was that the attraction was reciprocated.

'Whenever it happened the feeling seemed to be mutual. They obviously concluded that I was a lesbian, but the majority of them were perfectly normal, straight females so what did they see in me? It was frightening and extremely difficult to fathom out.'

That these women saw in Anne her masculinity was too much to hope for.

But beyond the initial admission of attraction, Anne was not prepared to tread.

'I began to think, perhaps I am a lesbian and that's what's really been wrong with me all the time.'

But although she felt very close to some women, she was always sufficiently wary to keep her distance. She never pursued them sexually, she just did not want to.

'I couldn't understand why I felt this fondness and attraction yet didn't want to do anything about it.'

The sexual enigma deepened as Anne's confusion mounted.

'It was as if I needed a name tag for myself, a label. Was I a woman, a lesbian, a bisexual, or a man? Things were no longer as clear cut as I'd imagined.'

While the very nature of her sexuality was being put to the test, Anne's marriage remained a needy prop for her growing insecurity. But despite the social niceties, the two were growing further and further apart.

Outwardly things looked fine; the teacher and his social worker wife would regularly dine with two or three other young professional married couples.

The talk was invariably of trivialities; work, how the house was going. For Anne it was a pleasant enough diversion from her secret nagging fears.

But in reality things were going badly wrong. They were becoming less and less open, as if in growing up together they had also outgrown one another. As if by way of gesture to that effect, Anne decided to revert to her maiden name of Johnson.

73

'I was fed up of being called Biddulph, I s'pose I didn't want to acknowledge that I was married and as it was the time when women started calling themselves "Ms", and it wasn't illegal to call yourself by your own name, I decided to set the trend.'

Andrew appeared indifferent to the move, not that he was given any real choice in the matter, and bank accounts, tax sheets, university and work registers were duly altered.

One question over which Anne was adamant was that of starting a family.

'We discussed having children and I always said no, no way was I going to have them. I didn't feel able to be a mother and bring up a child and I knew that if I opted out of looking after it, he wouldn't do it.

'I didn't want the responsibility, I would've gone berserk.'

Those were the arguments Anne repeatedly made against the notion. But she never confessed to Andrew the real reason.

'He was very straight, very much against homosexuality and anything perverse. I couldn't discuss my feelings towards women with him and as to anything further, well how could I possibly begin?'

So Anne continued to live within herself, at the same time questioning more and more her role as a woman and as a wife.

The turning point came with Anne's return to university. She was accepted on a course at Keele University, a redbrick establishment in Staffordshire, on a two year study for social workers. It meant an 80-mile round trip every day, but it was a chance to get back into student life and professionally Anne could not refuse. Not that she wanted to. She yearned for stimulation and this course was based much on the concept of self-analysis and self-awareness. It proffered the view that a good social worker needed to examine and know his or her own personality and to use it as a tool; for in questioning your own persona you would realize your own strengths and limitations, your ability to hold and influence others and to react to situations. This was the underlying theme and Anne was to find it profoundly disturbing. The course unit numbered twenty four students, which allowed for a generous amount of intimacy and Anne soon made friends. She and two of the other girls, Janet and Brenda, commuted daily from Birmingham and together they formed a car pool, meeting at a service station on the M6 motorway and travelling the rest of the journey in one car. It helped pay for the petrol and gave them a chance to discuss their work as they travelled.

Anne was still searching vainly for a label; her attraction to women, and theirs to her, showing no signs of abating. The old bugbear, lesbianism, continued, but while her fellow students were liberated they were not that way inclined. Only once was she approached with an eye to sex.

'As the course progressed, Janet became very fond of me, she would cuddle up to me in the lecture room. But once while we were sitting talking she said, almost jokingly, "Lesbe friends". At that point I found myself going off her, truly that was the last thing I wanted, it never felt right to imagine myself as a lesbian.'

Much more satisfying was her friendship with Heather, an American with a house near the university. It was Heather's superior intellect that Anne admired and they would spend much of their time studying together. It was she who introduced Anne to the books of Carlos Castinados, an anthropologist whose work dealt with evil forces, the powers of possession and the supernatural. Anne found them fascinating and took them home for Andrew to read. She thought no more about it at the time, for there was much to be done if she was to get to grips with her studies.

The self-analysis continued relentlessly and it was becoming increasingly difficult for Andrew to understand.

'It seemed to me that she'd become exposed to some pretty weird and wonderful things, cult things and encounter groups as in California. She started to knock any kind of normal behaviour, anything ordinary – and I'm afraid when she came home and told me what they'd been up to I'd laugh my head off.'

His derision hardly brought them any closer, and Anne's total preoccupation with herself and her studies meant that in comparison to life at Keele, home was rather boring. Nevertheless, the stimulation of argument had not entirely deserted them, and if their scientific and moral outlooks clashed it was still an interesting enough battle of wills.

Despite the intensity of the course, Anne's self-doubts came no nearer to resolving themselves, her course of action no clearer.

Questioning her every motivation only highlighted the contrast between herself and the other women and made the appreciation of them deeper. Participating in encounter groups proved revealing.

Paired off with Heather, she was told to massage her partner's feet, the object being to develop trust and reliance on others.

As Heather lay down, Anne began the massage.

'It was a very strange sensation, a feeling so strong that my hands began to shake, I was trembling so much. It was the first time I'd ever felt that intensely. I couldn't cope with it at all.'

Heather became aware of her trembling.

'She sat up and asked me what was wrong. I said I didn't know, and I really didn't have a clue what was going on.'

If Anne's emotions were now exposed, her subconscious would still not admit that, far from being peculiar, this was the normal reaction, the natural chemistry at work between male and female. Yet in the very next encounter group Heather was to pinpoint the characteristics in Anne that so many of her female friends had recognized and valued before.

'Who,' asked the professor, 'would you most like to be with if a disaster struck?' To Anne's surprise, Heather chose her.

'She said she felt that I was inwardly strong and that she knew she could rely on me, trust me to look after her, much as a man would.'

Anne reflected that she did indeed feel strong and protective towards the others, and that they were inclined to look to her for a lead.

Could it be that their attraction to her was plainly heterosexual? That her masculinity was somehow indefinably apparent to their female eyes? It was too much for her.

Yet as the course neared an end an odd occurrence left Anne further perplexed. In the last encounter group experiment, Janet and Brenda were found fighting, tearing one another's coats in obvious temper. Asked to analyse their anger – for by now everyone's motivations were automatically questioned – they confessed to being jealous of one another's relationship with Anne.

With Keele over it was as if life for Anne would never be the same again. She was better equipped now as a qualified social worker, but in personal terms, life had opened up as she had never thought possible.

Both she and Andrew recognized that the gulf between them

had grown enormous, but as yet neither were ready to voice their fears and go their separate ways. Instead, they began to pursue their lives independently, sharing little beyond a roof and a bed.

Only later was Anne to discover the agonies her husband was suffering; agonies which had begun with those borrowed books, the works of Don Carlos Castinados, and which were soon to rival her personal torture in their horror and complexity.

9

Eugene needed new sparring gloves and now that he had the cash to pay for them he went in search of the best available. He found them in a nondescript sportshop run from above Lloyds Bank in Bearwood High Street, Birmingham.

While browsing through the martial arts literature, he fell into conversation with the shopkeeper, Tim Ward, who was himself making a name in Kung Fu circles, both as a writer and as the owner of several local clubs.

Tim was impressed by Eugene's knowledge and realizing he might be able to capitalize on such expertise, he invited Eugene and his brother to look in on his classes.

There was an ulterior motive: for two years Tim had employed a Chinese family, the Hos, as instructors. But old Mr Ho and his son, Toby, were demanding more money for their services and Tim was not one to give in.

'I was looking for someone with ability to take over from the Hos, and the Lungs, as they introduced themselves, seemed to fit the bill.'

As Eugene talked in a style resembling David Carradine and his brother with a convincing American accent, the fact that they claimed to have just returned from the States – where they had been training with none other than Bruce Lee himself – all sounded plausible enough, taking into account their impressive skills.

'I was inclined to believe them, watching them doing double swords probably better than most people I had seen in my travels all over the world. Very few people could do that.'

Tim Ward's classes were held in various halls and centres throughout the city, usually on Wednesdays and at weekends.

Taking up his invitation, the brothers ventured to the Sunday class in Bourneville Church Hall, next to the giant Cadbury's chocolate factory. Eugene was not impressed by what he saw.

'There was very little discipline, half the time seemed to be spent in drinking tea or smoking. There were about thirty-five lads in the class and really they were just clowning around, they could easily have kicked one another's brains in.'

Suspicious of the Lungs, the older of the two Chinese asked the brothers to demonstrate what they could do. They chose the long-range circling and attacking techniques of the White Crane, the Bok Hok Pai. The Hos were suitably impressed, but when Eugene offered to engage them in a friendly spar they took it as a threat and declined.

Realizing they were likely to be usurped, they warned him, in fractured English, that the school was no good, Mr Ward owed them money and they were being financially ripped off. Eugene in turn told Tim that his school was hopeless. Tim's scheme had worked.

'The only alternative to packing it all in, which I was reluctant to do although I knew the Hos were on their way out, was to offer Eugene the chance to take over. To my relief he agreed, for a while at least.'

So the Lungs, as they were now commonly known, found themselves full-time instructors in charge of the Chinese Martial Arts Centre.

Initially, as Tim remembers to his cost, Eugene proved to be bad for business.

'He was so good that the training he gave was too hard for most of the pupils. They had a natural tendency to be slack, but to survive with Eugene they had to have the mentality to succeed. Not a minute of classtime was wasted, and in that respect he gave good value for money.'

Nonetheless, an initial forty-five minutes of rigorous stamina training followed by strictly regimented sets was enough to deter the majority of Eugene's first class. Out of fifty, only twenty students returned the following week.

At last Eugene had his chance to assert his authority, to exert his power over the men for whom he had come to have scant regard.

'I told them, I was in control and I wanted to see them suffer for their own good. Without suffering they would never become expert.'

His obsession with fitness and discipline had reached the level of paranoia. He harnessed their mental and physical abilities in strict military fashion, something that he doubtless had instilled in him at the Irish training school.

'I insisted they marshalled in straight lines, kept quiet and reacted immediately to my every instruction. It was the only way to get results.'

For encouragement, the Lungs would give frequent demonstrations of sparring and weapon fighting. It was awe-inspiring stuff and induced much hero worship.

If Eugene demanded dedication from his students, his self-discipline was reaching extremes. His body was now so finely tuned through exercise that fact and fiction became completely interwoven.

'I don't know of anyone who did more exercise than Eugene', says Tim. 'He had a range that was astounding, I've never seen anyone with greater flexibility.'

Flexible in body meant flexible in mind and as his loyal students took to dubbing him Master, so he became convinced that he was, indeed, Chinese.

A lifetime of roleplay and pretence was captured in the mysterious upbringing Master E. C. Lung invented for himself. Sifu Lung was born not in that Armagh hospital to poacher stock, but in the far more glamorous Wan Chi district of Hong Kong. While his parents were European, his father in the army (both true enough), he was brought up by his godfather one Master Chak Fu Lung, who taught his protégé Kung Fu from the age of four. He spoke little English, hence the clipped Carradine impersonation, his native tongues being Mandarin and Cantonese. Such was the tale that Eugene told; a smoke-screen of wishful thinking that, thanks to his undoubted talent, speech patterns and oriental mode of dress, became credible.

It says much for the force of his personality at the time that his family corroborated this romantic fairytale.

'Michael was as involved in martial arts as I was so it was natural that he should go along with me. My parents had long given up trying to understand me, and so if it made me feel better to think I was Chinese, then that was okay with them.'

As for the Mandarin and Cantonese, both the Lungs had picked up a passable understanding from their Chinese friends. But this was no clever hoodwink. Concentrated breathing, yoga and hours of transcendental meditation had finally been rewarded and at last Eugene had attained that most elusive of powers, the Chi Kung.

'I felt myself in complete control of my mental and physical strength. For once in my life I was completely in tune.'

His cabaret was pure magic, as Tim Ward witnessed.

'Chi Kung gives a tremendous strength and on many occasions I saw him push genuinely lethal, sharp swords against his throat until they bent in two. He could bang a stick hard against his body and it'd snap in half but he didn't feel a thing; he'd make his stomach swell up hard and no matter how hard you hit him he wouldn't be hurt.

'Sometimes he would touch people very lightly and they would jump back across the room, yet he'd hardly made contact with them. It was incredible to watch.'

For Eugene it was the ultimate achievement.

'It was such a spiritual power, I felt so strong within. It was as if nothing could hurt me ever again.'

But spectacular though all this was, it could be directly attributed to his intensive training in the martial arts. Other abilities were less easily explained and expert opinion regarding his techniques with the White Crane and Wu Su was somewhat divided, as Tim explains:

'The karate higher grades were certainly interested in Eugene. They'd ask me how he had learned techniques of theirs which were not readily available.

'It struck me that often he seemed to have more knowledge than the experts themselves, but I haven't a clue where he got it from.

'A lot of people in the business scoffed, but in terms of what he and Michael could do, there was no way they could've simply picked it all up from books.'

No indeed, countered Eugene. For had he not been brought up in the Buddhist tradition and spent fourteen of his formative years mastering the most difficult of the martial arts? But if that was all pure fantasy, just how could he explain his extraordinary skills, his knowledge of movements rarely witnessed in the West and which could hardly be the result of an overworked imagination?

In truth the intense periods of meditation and his complete absorption with the spiritualism of his craft had revived the instinctive, visionary powers which had enabled him to picture Hong Kong so clearly.

'Things came to me in a flash, the power was like a mind video, a huge cinema screen. The sound was stereo and I was watching and listening. There was no warning and once it was there it'd only go away of its own accord.'

Call it second sight, but Eugene claims it was this strange force that gave him access to much he knew, in particular to Taichi, the supreme ultimate fists.

In Ling T'Sun or Wing Chun, most experts can perform the three common sets; it was, says Eugene, the visions that taught him the two additional, advanced moves that few people know of. When he spoke of travelling in Tibet with the Shaolin monks, describing in elaborate detail their way of summoning the Yeti with bells, Tim Ward was sceptical.

'He would natter on about it and about philosophies of Buddhism and so forth, I didn't really believe a word. He talked about these underground caves where he'd seen work on advanced and secret technology in operation. I'd laugh and imagine he was pulling my leg.'

It was not until 1980 that Eugene's "journey" and his extra-ordinary sightseeing were verified.

In California doing some journalistic research, Tim was granted an interview with a martial arts expert, a genuine Shaolin monk. In conversation, the monk told Tim the very same stories.

'When I replicd that I'd already heard of these things and told him about Eugene, he was astounded. He said these things had happened two hundred and fifty years ago and couldn't possibly be known to a Caucasian.'

In practical terms, the psychic powers enabled Eugene to perform feats and party tricks in the mode of Uri Geller. He frequently stopped clocks by staring at them hard, restarting them by turning his back.

Travelling one day in Tim's Ford Capri to a club some fifteen miles away in the new town of Redditch, Eugene's hand was shaking badly after a prolonged period of attaining Chi Kung.

'He reached for the air nozzle to cool himself down, but the intense heat of his body simply melted the chrome off in his hands. He didn't panic, but it seemed most weird.'

Now that Sifu Lung was in control and the world seemed inclined to believe him, Eugene felt momentarily at peace within his personal gender trap.

The height of this glorious respite from reality came with magazine articles and subsequent television appearances.

"Sifu Lung, the Master of the White Crane, is unique in this country in that he is expert in several Kung Fu styles and specializes in no fewer than thirty-five Kung Fu weapons," proclaimed an article in *Fighter*. "What's more, he specializes in acupuncture, herbal medicine and Chinese painting." After an impressive list of his martial arts skills, we learn that: "During a typical training day under his godfather, Sifu Lung would be awakened at five a.m., practising Taichi, Chang-Chuan and practical fighting for up to five hours. After his training he would then have breakfast and go to school. A day's work already!

"A further six hours of training occupied his evenings, a typical day's work which was to continue for fourteen years. It was only after he had reached his peak, at the age of twenty that he was reunited with his parents and his brother.

"They returned from their travels abroad and he went to live with them in San Francisco before moving to New York and eventually returning to Honk Kong and from there to England." It concluded: "There are very few White Crane Masters in this country and Sifu Lung must be the only Master able to use the fourteen weapons of this system and also demonstrate its fourteen hundred moves."

Even Eugene himself was agreeably impressed.

10

Returning to the reality of life in the raw – for that was how it presented itself in the daily catalogue of distress Anne dealt with in her casework – did nothing to lessen the self-doubts which had emerged at Keele.

If anything her sensitivities were more finely tuned than ever before, her preference for women becoming an overwhelming preoccupation and a burdensome worry.

She had won her battle for a white sports car, a souped up Sunbeam Alpine which seemed to symbolize the sense of freedom she was now constantly yearning for.

Andrew was confused. 'She was as free as anyone could be, I really held no restraint on her. The car had been the first thing I'd said no to, but she had to win in the end didn't she?'

Anne was by no means alone in her search for a new approach and attitude to herself and to womanhood in general. Up and down the country women of her generation were in the throes of questioning their role in society, demanding equality and freedom of choice with a common voice not heard so loudly since their great grandmothers won for all British women the right to vote.

Action groups in support of the Women's Liberation Movement were strident in their attack. Equal pay and opportunities, sexual freedoms, and more materially, rights of property, were the issues they fought for and which were to take more than a decade to achieve. If the liberationists were labelled extremists, their battlecry penetrated to the silent majority of females and struck a chord that was to alter attitudes more fundamentally than anyone had realized.

But it was the bra-burning, banner-waving women who led

the way and made the headlines, with the Press unflagging in their pursuit.

Within the field of social work there were many women whose political inclinations – progressive left-wing – and ideals made them eager supporters of Women's Lib.

Anne was eager to find out more, seizing ever hopefully on it as another possible answer to her predicament.

Fresh from the intellectual stimulus of Keele, she found plenty to theorize abut with her new colleagues, in particular with a girl called Penny, herself fiercely committed to the Movement.

Penny lived in the once fashionable area of Birmingham called Moseley. In its prime during the Victorian era, it still held the charm of the village it had been long ago, but now its attraction was broader, bohemian even, as the influx of students and immigrants mixed in a rich and exciting cosmopolitan cocktail.

She shared a house with two girls of similar views and for Anne it became a refuge from her disenchantment. As with Heather, the attraction to Penny was intellectual rather than physical. Nevertheless, to Andrew the alienation from Anne that he was feeling more and more nowadays was heightened by her attachment to this particular group of friends. Like many men at the time he was bewildered and at times let the pain he felt manifest itself as anger and derision.

'She had got in with the wrong crowd, I don't know if they were lesbians but they seemed loose to me, morally that is. They used to go and drink together in this dreadful pub. They called themselves liberationists and they'd certainly liberated themselves from the housework as far as I could see. Anne dragged me to a party there once, I can only describe it as a tip. I wasn't happy about her mixing with them at all. I suppose I'd become a pretty stay-at-home sort of bloke, but they seemed to be giving her all sorts of ideas that I couldn't in all honesty go along with.'

Despite his obvious disapproval, or maybe even because of it, Anne began to spend more of her time in their company. The aims and ideals of the Liberation Movement were never more of an issue than when it came down to basic everyday problems.

'I suppose we were always going on about it at work, sticking up for our rights. We moved a great heavy desk once, Penny and I. All the secretaries in the office wanted us to wait and ask the men to do it, they said the men were stronger and we'd do ourselves an injury.

'It was ridiculous really, but we were determined to show them we could do it just as well, so between us we humped this huge thing down two flights of stairs. We didn't admit it to anyone of course, but we were absolutely exhausted and aching all over, but we enjoyed every second of it.'

Such demonstrations of equality were small measure compared to the serious issues up for discussion at the liberation meetings which Penny persuaded Anne to attend. But while she willingly gave up wearing a bra – 'I'd never felt right or comfortable in the damn things anyway, so this was just a grand excuse to abandon them forever' – she was somehow hesitant to pledge herself wholeheartedly.

'I was very interested in what they had to say, but although I had every sympathy with what they were trying to achieve – and there really was no argument I could see against liberation – I just didn't feel at home there among all those women.

'I wanted to be one of them, to benefit from their demands by being successful, but somehow the movement itself, well, I just didn't feel it was for me.'

Anne's friends were not the only ones puzzled by her reaction; she herself found it more worrying than she cared to admit.

'What was wrong with me? I wanted freedom, independence, not just from the world I'd created around me, my marriage and all, but from the chaos inside me that was constantly churning away.

'I knew that I was looking for something and I knew that somewhere I just had to find it, but Women's Lib, well that wasn't it.'

But why not: why could she identify with but not fully commit herself to this cause? Was it not this sisterhood that she had been seeking through the undisputed attraction to other women? She had already rejected lesbianism – was she now to reject women's liberation as an answer to her problems? It was inevitable that Anne would find the environment of Women's Lib ambiguous, and she quickly recognized the reasons.

'I secretly knew that the reason I couldn't become fully

involved was that my feelings inside just weren't that of a female, they weren't in any way feminine. Yes, I could sympathize and up to a point support them, but to be seen as a woman, fighting together with the rest for the rights of womanhood, was alien to how I felt and I knew myself to be inside. And it was there somewhere, within me, that the identification I had with women simply came to a stop.'

Once again Anne had tried to find an outlet for her frustrations and failed. For in her truly honest moments, Anne realized that what she wanted to see was not simply liberation for women, but for everyone, so that in determining their personal sexual role each man and woman could be free to live openly as they chose.

In the meantime her peace of mind had once again been badly shaken. Frightened to allow the feelings of masculinity any expression, Anne compromised herself by maintaining a peripheral interest in both her liberated women friends and her husband.

But the Andrew she stuck somewhat half-heartedly to for some vestige of security was not the man she had grown up with and married. Nor was he merely the long-suffering, home-loving husband she imagined. For just as Anne had always kept from him her awesome doubts and suspicions, so Andrew had begun to keep things close to his chest, secrets that he was equally reluctant to share.

What Anne did not know was that her innocent attempt to involve him in her life at Keele, by bringing home books she thought he would enjoy, had enmeshed him in a web of power that was slowly and imperceptibly changing his whole personality.

Don Carlos Castinados, the anthropologist who had fascinated Anne with his tales of North Mexican Indians, their black magic and witchcraft, had presented a challenge to Andrew. As a rational scientist he was intrigued by the idea of a force with supernatural powers, in particular the power of possession.

In theory Castinados' book purported to embody a neutral force, which could only be attained by first cutting oneself off from others and from all worldly preoccupations. By looking, as it were, at the spaces between the leaves on a tree rather than at the leaves themselves, the student would be touched somehow by the power which apparently filled the universe.

Eventually, after no less than ten or even fifteen years of persevering, the student would become a sorcerer's apprentice and would have the full power to use as he chose. For the force was neutral and the choice was his to use for good or for evil. But to reach that stage it was vital to first become a warrior, to identify with the power and to sublimate himself to the force. It was strong stuff, but compelling reading. Almost in spite of himself Andrew had decided to test some of Castinados' theories.

'It didn't ring true, wasn't rational and so to me it was something of a scientific challenge if you like. But I really didn't have a clue what I was letting myself in for.'

Andrew began his tentative experiments with the force while working as a full-time chemist. For if the workload was heavy, the laboratory relaxed at lunchtime by playing bridge and, to his amazement, Andrew discovered that he could control the game and thus his own fortune.

It was the same with dice games: his powers of concentration meant the numbers fell as if to his command. Harmless though it seemed, Andrew realized the implications; but he was loath to stop.

'Once I started experimenting it seemed to gain its own momentum, it gave me a tremendous power to affect other people's actions. My own stupid ego began to build up and I started to believe that it was me doing all these things, using my own natural abilities. It was stupid, I didn't like or want to admit that it was the weird power.'

For some twelve months as the powers grew stronger Andrew had kept his experiments to himself.

Now, as Anne questioned why he was grown so distant, he began to reveal his preoccupations, even giving her glimpses of what he could do.

'There was a flower pot up on a shelf, high it was, just above the curtain rail. As I watched he made it lift and move across, it seemed to float, it was like telekinesis, all he had to do was look at it. I didn't know what to think.

'Then he told me about the dice and the bridge school, and about a random digital display at work, that he could alter the numbers just by concentrating.'

If at first it all seemed like some clever trickery, an attempt by Andrew to show his supremacy over her, Anne gradually recognized that there was far more to it than that.

Both remained confirmed atheists. From Anne's point of view, 'Nobody could show me God and I couldn't understand how there could be one with so many terrible things going on in the world. I didn't believe in God at all. For a start, if He did exist why had He given me the wrong body?

'I vaguely believed there could be ghosts and strange spirits and I felt there was most definitely a force at work somewhere in the universe, maybe an evil force. While Andrew kept insisting it was only a neutral power he had, it was something I began to wish he hadn't got in touch with at all.'

But it was too late; Andrew seemed to be taking a gleeful delight in his newfound strengths, even gloating in his achievements.

Anne was frustrated by it all. She was equally fascinated, but however much she wanted to believe and to achieve the power she did not seem able to get anywhere.

But the full extent of Andrew's power was as yet unrevealed. The first inkling came that summer, when to bury their differences they set out on holiday.

Since their student days both had preferred to spend these breaks in active pursuit of the outdoor life; indeed Anne had been walking and climbing up Mount Snowdon and even to Ben Nevis.

This time they set out to walk the Pennine Way, the very backbone of England. Travelling by train to its northernmost point, they planned to walk south down the Way and into Derbyshire.

Anne was looking forward to the exercise, the fresh air and the chance for some peaceful contemplation. Out in the open, dressed in the rugged gear essential for the British climate, she felt more at one with herself. She was admittedly unfit, but the many walking holidays she had experienced in the past were far more arduous than this promised to be.

The train journey was uneventful, but as they reached their destination and set out on foot, Anne found herself collapsing under the weight of her rucksack. Both she and Andrew were carrying heavy loads, but that was usual on such trips. Anne had always prided herself on her ability to manage as much as Andrew, a token proof she was as good as any man. Now she found herself hardly able to put one foot in front of the other.

'I felt really most peculiar, as if there was a ton of weight on my head crushing me down, I could hardly walk. Andrew stood there, laughing out loud at me, but I could almost see him thinking, "There you are, I've shown you, we're not as equal as you like to think."

'I couldn't understand why this was happening, really my rucksack wasn't that heavy at all.'

For the rest of the day Anne struggled to keep pace with Andrew, stumbling along behind him, feeling burdened and again inexplicably, severely depressed. By evening the rain had become torrential, a storm that brought visibility down to a few yards. The couple, usually adept at map reading and with a well-developed sense of direction, found themselves lost, unable to work out which way to turn next.

They both felt as if the elements had somehow combined with Andrew's imperceptible power, creating a heavy and intolerable pressure. Whatever the explanation, neither felt the events of that night to be wholly natural. Next morning, soaked through and exhausted from lack of sleep, they mutually agreed to abandon the Pennines.

Anne's depression had turned to sullen anger, but she was to have a holiday at all costs. Bundling tent and belongings into the back of the car, they set out in disgruntled silence for Wales and the beauty of the Gower coast.

It was to prove a miserable week, the first holiday each had gone their separate ways. For the majority of the time, Andrew explored the seashore, while Anne spent her days in splendid isolation, either reading in the tent of wandering alone along the coastal paths. The mood between them was distant, conversation virtually nil.

Anne's light reading, bought on impulse in a tiny Welsh bookshop, turned out to be a story of two homosexuals. She found it fascinating and spent most of the week totally absorbed within herself and the storyline.

At the weekend they decided to leave the coast and to drive into the Welsh mountains, equally spectacular with their sweeping scenery.

'That's when I found the valley. It took us both by surprise; Andrew had described it to me exactly earlier in the week. He said he'd had a flash, a sort of vision of this place, and there we were looking at a valley that sounded identical. We didn't know the area so it wasn't somewhere we recalled from memory. It made me quite jumpy.'

More than a little pleased with the growing power his dabbling with the occult had given him, Andrew became immediately talkative, enthusing about the tales of power attributed to the Indians.

'He decided to experiment. The Indians had sat for hours on the rocks, so he did the same while I dozed.'

It was extraordinarily hot; they had left the car parked up on the road, the tent was pitched a couple of hundred yards away. They camped for three days and nights, Anne growing more tense with the oppressive heat and the strange effect of being enclosed in the valley.

'I can't explain it even now, but it was as if there was a powerful presence watching us. Andrew seemed to feel it too, but to him it was exhilarating.

'There was no doubt he thought he was going to become a warrior and that he was following the path of power. We both knew it, but we didn't talk about it.'

Anne was once again confused and not a little jealous of his apparent power. Her reasoning told her not to be so foolish, what was happening to Andrew could hardly be desirable.

'I felt it could only be an evil influence that he was under, because it implied that to achieve power you had to stop loving and caring about everything and everyone, in other words completely cut yourself off. Although Andrew couldn't see it himself at the time, that was what was happening to him; he was beginning to keep himself from everyone.'

All things considered it was no surprise that the holiday had proven disastrous. On the last night of their stay the car was broken into and Anne's temper was hardly improved by hordes of midges, aroused by the dust and the heat, so thick they swarmed around their noses, even in their mouths. To Anne it seemed as though an omen of the evil was embodied all around them, even in Andrew.

She drove them home, belligerent and tense. The holiday she had been looking forward to had been ruined. She felt inevitably that it was the end of the road for her tired marriage.

'He could sense what I was feeling, I was so angry there was no need for us to say anything. He was blaming me too for the car being broken into.'

Anne, after school, aged 11

Anne poses for the family snapshot in the garden

Tomboy Anne is forced into a flowery dress and a perm

Eugene's early attempts at model making

Eugene practising the ancient art of Kung Fu

Eugene performs *Wing Chun* with a pupil

Michael, Eugene's brother, performs *White Crane fist* in front of an audience
in Birmingham

Eugene relaxes himself mentally before his physical exertions

Anne at the time of her marriage to Andrew

Eugene (senior) and May Brown with their grand-daughter, Emma

An early shot of Eugene and Anne

Baby Emma

Cathy, Emma and Chris

Emma with her parents

She was at bursting point, and the aggravation she felt at her own inadequacies, at Andrew's current glee in winning one over on her came tumbling out.

'I told him I was leaving him, I was going. Not that I had anywhere to go or anyone to stay with except my parents, and that didn't seem like a good idea.'

Andrew looked suddenly down in the mouth. Now that Anne had finally spoken her mind she felt upset too.

'I felt that if he was going to continue to be influenced by this evil power, there was no way I wanted to stay with him on those terms.'

For the breakdown in their marriage was more than simply a case of childhood sweethearts who were admitting to having married too soon, before their adult ideas and individual persona had had a chance to fully develop.

They were being pulled apart by far stronger influences and circumstances – Andrew by psychic forces he himself could hardly grasp, Anne by her irrevocable inner feelings. Now that the dissent between them had been voiced they were left in something of a vacuum.

Yet when it came to the point of actually finding somewhere else to live, Anne's resolve melted.

'I was extremely low and for once it just got the better of me. For the first time in ages I was crying because of the frustration of not knowing what to do.'

Despite their differences, Andrew had given her security which even now she was reluctant to lose. To stay, knowing there was precious little left between them, was hardly a better alternative.

'For the first time I realized I didn't really have any life with him anymore, that as far as I was concerned there really was no reason for living with him.'

Andrew remains cynical about his wife's reasoning.

'She'd thought I was under her control, that she'd always have things her own way, but it had got to the stage where I wasn't. There were so many things happening to me; I felt she resented that very much.'

If their relationship had become little more than a habit to her, it was still the easy option and one which however unstable, was a safety net:

'I asked him if he still loved me; he said, yes, he did, and I said something stupid about how if we did split up, what would I tell my mother. One way or another, I agreed to stay.'

As Anne, once again, withdrew into herself, their sexual relationship became increasingly difficult and eventually ceased altogether.

If there was an alienation between them, living in the same cottage did not help. Anne had never liked the place and now, whether through resentment, imagination or a genuine fear she found it menacing and depressing.

'I could never get warm. If I sat in the chair it felt icy cold, the same with the couch. It was always so dark and gloomy.'

The atmosphere seemed to be affecting her three cats too, for they appeared terrified whenever they came indoors.

'For some reason Andrew started to call the place Armageddon. I began to feel there was definitely something peculiar going on, there was a strange atmosphere that wasn't there before. I wasn't so much afraid as intensely irritated.'

In the vain hope of overcoming whatever was causing the tension, Anne made frantic plans to alter the house, changing the furniture around and drawing up plans for an extension. Andrew set about digging a huge hole for the foundations.

All this time it had remained a weekly ritual to visit Anne's parents on Wednesday for tea, a meal followed by the avid viewing of a Kung Fu series currently being televised. Anne became a fan, and when she then saw Bruce Lee's box office blockbuster, *Enter the Dragon*, her tomboyish spirit, which had never deserted her, was caught up.

'I knew a girl who did karate, but that didn't appeal to me at all. It was Kung Fu that had taken hold of my mind.'

It was pure coincidence that Tony Ho should choose this time to advertise the Chinese Martial Arts Centre in the local *Evening Mail*. Anne was tempted to join the evening classes; if nothing more it would surely be a welcome outlet for her frustrations at the way life was going. Andrew was wryly amused:

'But I think she did it more to counter me, I think she'd grown wary and frightened of me even, and this would teach her some sort of defence.'

Whatever the reasoning Anne joined the Wednesday evening class held at the Friends' Meeting House hall in Hay Mills, being the most convenient to both work and home.

She was not alone in being lured along by the advertisements. There were other newcomers that evening; two girls, Nita and Liz, a young married bank clerk with whom over the weeks Anne was to strike up a firm friendship.

'I liked Anne; she struck me as a kind and gentle person. I s'pose you'd say she was a tomboyish sort of girl, she didn't wear a bra or makeup, no perfume or anything like that, and she said she never wore anything but trousers. But she was a fairly cheerful person and we got on well together, seeing as how we started at the same time. After the class we'd be dying of thirst so we used to go for a quick drink on our way home.'

While they both enjoyed their lessons they found the Chinese teacher difficult to follow and it was a job to keep up. They needed to practise and after a few weeks Anne invited Liz to the cottage so that they could work together in the garden.

Andrew watched in amusement as the pair practised their sequences with two large poles, prancing around the lawn avoiding the vegetable patch.

Says Liz: 'We would never be good enough to fight properly, but we were certainly getting fit, toning up our arm and leg muscles.'

Her impressions of the Biddulph household remained vivid.

'Andrew struck me as having something of the mad scientist about him. He was wearing shorts and sandals and was digging this vast hole which he said he was going to fill with chicken manure to make his own gas. There was a big tank too and he told me he was about to build an extension. They seemed to be in a state of upheaval; Anne's sports car was in the drive with a Rover Andrew was fixing, all in bits.'

As for their relationship:

'I always felt that they were just good friends, as they say, nothing like a love match or anything, they were more old familiars.'

The visit was repeated and Liz met Anne's father, busying himself helping Andrew.

'They seemed very close, Anne and her Dad. He was such a nice man and obviously enjoyed being with her.'

Just as the girls' enthusiasm for the martial arts began to develop with their increasing confidence, so the rift between Tim Ward and the Ho family finally erupted.

'It was quite a dust up,' Anne recalls. 'We weren't sure what would happen. But Tim told us not to worry, he'd found someone else, a new and better teacher.'

IIc arrived the following week, introducing himself as none other than Master E. C. Sifu Lung.

11

For Eugene the visionary powers which had haunted him since childhood had brought not only an acute perception of the ways of ancient China and Tibet, but also a recurring image of a female, which in reality had so far eluded him. The picture was of a woman, taller than himself, kindly and apparently intelligent, who appeared either poring over books in study or marching in protest. The detail was blurred, but Eugene recalls knowing that the woman was a student, and at university. It was an image upon which he had placed little importance, but since his late teens it had appeared with such regularity that he subconsciously began searching for a parallel in real life.

As the Hay Mills class lined up for the first time, teacher and pupils eyed each other warily. Eugene's diminutive figure in his loose tunic and with his long hair cut in oriental fringed fashion, took some by surprise, the only hint of his physical strength being his short but muscular arms. They were soon to learn that Sifu – the Master – was a formidable character who belied his outward appearance. Eugene's power lay in his speed and agility which more than made up for any lack of physical stature.

Moreover, he was severe with idlers and stragglers and from that first encounter insisted on the iron discipline which he had established in the rest of the school.

He began as he meant to go on; the class were to bow when he entered, to treat him with the deference due to all Masters of Kung Fu. Aware that he had their full and curious attention, Eugene's sense of the theatrical came into play; as he took the centre stage, his pupils circled around him. For half an hour the Master told his tale: of being brought up by his godfather from the age of three, of his Chinese childhood, his exclusive training in the martial arts.

He impressed on them the wonderful powers of Kung Fu, even throwing in a brief but spectacular demonstration of his incredible swordbending, so encouraging them to copy what to most sounded and seemed impossible.

Their enthusiasm, which had flagged somewhat with the uncertainties generated by the departure of the Hos, was replenished by Eugene's peptalk. Wasting no time that evening, they eagerly fell in to show him their skills, meagre in some, promising in others.

All had been affected and impressed by their new teacher, who clearly intended to make their classes a worthwhile if demanding proposition from everyone's point of view.

Liz and Anne started their faltering sets of White Crane, painfully aware of their own inadequacies, as Eugene began to walk round, mentally noting individual abilities.

He was confidently aware that he had managed to inspire his new class, to win their initial respect and admiration. As yet he had no notion of the impact he had made on one pupil in particular, namely Anne.

'The moment I saw him I was absolutely fascinated. I was attracted, very attracted indeed. But I'd only ever felt interested in two or-three men in my entire life up to that point, including Andrew. And more recently it'd been women that I'd found attractive. How could I be drawn to both? It was all racing through my mind.

'But then, looking at Eugene, watching him, I suddenly had this weird insight. There was a man – or was it a man? Somehow the person I was looking at so intently seemed more like a woman. He attracted me as a woman might, not like a man at all!'

It was a strangely exhilarating experience, one that filled her with an unnerving excitement. She found it impossible to concentrate.

Eugene reached the small group of women, his mind pre-occupied with the shapes and forms of the White Crane. Scanning their faces he set eyes on Anne – and was abruptly jolted from his thoughts. Here at last was the woman who had appeared to him so often, the human replica of the visionary

98

figure he knew so well – or thought he did. Had it been a dream?

That was not all. Several of his women pupils had made it obvious they found him interesting, but their feelings had never been reciprocated. Far from it. Eugene found it extremely painful to watch them performing the martial arts, presenting an image which he himself longed to have. The hard discipline he insisted upon from his male pupils was therefore applied equally to the women; it was some retribution for being trapped within his detested masculine frame.

But here was a woman he found disturbingly different.

'I immediately fancied her, which was strange in itself. I thought from the way she looked that maybe she was the liberated type, maybe a lesbian.

'But then I was struck by one thought – it's not a she! It's a guy! I know it's a guy! Somehow I felt certain she was a man, it was a dominating presence and I was sure I was right. I just knew, don't ask me how, that she was different from all the others, and it threw me completely.'

It was a unique coincidence, but there was no time to take things further on that first evening. Not that either of them was ready to explore their respective and equally disturbing thoughts. The awareness had been mutual and both knew it to be so.

Anne's elation carried her home, spilling out as she recounted to Andrew the arrival of the new teacher and the antics he got up to, carefully omitting any detail of her personal fascination.

'I felt that there was definitely something spiritual about him and it was that I knew would interest Andrew. The whole thing was buzzing in my head, I couldn't really understand why I'd reacted to Sifu Lung as I did, but it certainly made me feel marvellous.'

Both she and Eugene found themselves looking forward to the Wednesday lessons and within a couple of weeks it became apparent to everyone that the Master was incredibly interested in Anne Biddulph.

'They began to joke and say "Hey, c'mon we're all paying for these lessons you know, not just her". I didn't care, I couldn't help myself, I just found myself gravitating towards her every few minutes.

Liz too shared in some of Eugene's more individual attentions.

'He was a very theatrical person, he always wore the Chinese trousers and jacket, or he'd dress totally in black, slacks and a polo neck jumper. I never saw him in a shirt or a tie. He'd come over and talk to us, usually ranting on at a great rate in his funny clipped voice about things. He gave us both Tiger Balms; he kept a little cat box of the stuff which he swore by. He was always on about massage, if either of us said we had a headache he'd offer to massage it away.'

Yet Eugene could equally be frightening.

'He was only a little bloke but he wouldn't let you get away with much. He wasn't quite so bad with the girls but the blokes, he really used to crack down on them; if they were slacking he'd drag them out to the front and really let them have it.'

No one knew the real reasons for Eugene's bursts of aggression.

'I would look into the Hay Mills windows and catch reflections of the women doing their exercises – and it'd make me mad, so mad that I'd begin to boil. All I could do was to take it out on the others, I'd kick one of the fellows in the head, torment him, call him a damn fool and kick him until he was hurt. I'd get them to choose a partner and progress from a kick and punch. One night I was so mad I kicked this lad too hard and almost broke his arm.

'I couldn't help myself, I knew it was wrong but I felt so out of place, detested myself so much; to me my body was grotesque. It was agonizing to me, watching the women. The men thought I was violent out of frustration, because I fancied girls.'

Liz for one was left in no doubt that the Master was one hundred per cent hot-blooded male.

'I never gave a thought he was otherwise. I'd never seen anyone who could be so aggressive. In any case, he seemed to have his eye on Anne. He was so quick and flexible at Kung Fu, it was fantastic to watch, you couldn't help admiring him and wanting to do well for him.'

If there was any outward signs of Eugene's true feminine spirit they only took on any importance viewed in retrospect.

'He giggled a lot with us,' remembers Liz. 'If he was telling a story he'd lean on you, a bit like a girlfriend might do, it used to embarrass me.'

When it came to changing before and after class, Eugene

could never bear to join the men and found it difficult to resist the natural inclination to follow the women. Instead, he would disappear into the toilets to undress in privacy, or more disruptively, throw all the men out of the changing room while he got ready.

'I never wanted the men to see my body nor did I want to see theirs. I hated the very thought of mixing with them, of revealing myself, it seemed totally unnatural.'

At that time they put it down to his oriental upbringing; it was no more than another of the Master's little idiosyncracies and just added to his mysterious appeal.

In the meantime Anne was persevering in the gracious sets of the White Crane, but on her sweeping circling movements looked awkward and incongruous. To Eugene it was a positive pointer to Anne's masculinity.

'She was too stiff, not dainty like the other women. She had a very bad kneecap because of some cartilage trouble and it made her knee give way. I rubbed it for her and it gave me quite a shock. She didn't even feel like a female somehow. It was weird and I had a job pulling myself together.'

He did and switched Anne to Win Chun.

'That was much more her style, more static and direct, she got into the sets straight away.'

By now the attraction between Master and pupil was irresistible. The pretence at coolness could no longer be maintained. Eugene needed to know more about this woman who moved him so deeply and disconcertingly.

'I had to know and so eventually I plucked up the courage to ask her was she married? She said "yes" – then blurted out straight away: "but I'm leaving him". It was as if she wanted to reassure me that it didn't count, it didn't matter.'

For Anne it was the cue she had been longing for.

Hesitatingly she broached the question that had been on the tip of her tongue for weeks. Would Sifu, the Master, go out with her? It was an irrevocable step, but Anne was past caring. In Eugene she sensed a kindred spirit, a soul mate with whom she could somehow identify as with no one ever before.

Eugene was apprehensive but delighted. The rigorous physical and mental regime he had imposed on himself for so long had successfully numbed all sense of reality. Now the appearance of Anne had shaken him beyond all reason. Yet he felt instinctively that fate had taken him in hand, and while he was treading on dangerous ground, what had to be simply had to be.

Anne's feelings were equally mixed. She had never gone behind Andrew's back with another man and here she was launching on what augered to be a full-blown affair. But the promise that she sensed a relationship with Eugene had in store was far too inviting to overlook.

So their first date was arranged for two days hence – a Friday evening. Anne made suitable excuses to Andrew, hardly difficult given the amount of time they now spent following their own pursuits. Like two adolescents on their first date she and Eugene ventured out as a couple.

They met in the anonymity of the city centre, eating at an Indian restaurant and talking of China, of philosophies and ideals and discovering there was much that they had in common. Eugene was euphoric.

'It was terrific, just terrific. Because I knew that here I was eating out not with a girl but with a man, I felt marvellous. For the first time in my life I was being treated like a female, Anne seemed to know instinctively that was what I wanted.'

When it came to paying the bill, Eugene was embarrassed to find himself short of cash.

'Anne simply took over and without any fuss, settled up.'

Neither wanted the evening to end so soon, and it was Anne who suggested they take a walk by the canal basin. It was an oasis in the heart of the city, a place where she loved to wander among the houseboats, remembering with nostalgia the happier times of her own canal days.

The night was clear and suitably romantic and Eugene felt no surprise when Anne put her arm around him, holding him close. So they stood under the bridge, presenting to the world an incongruous sight, but too happy in their own oblivion to care. For both it was a moment almost too precious to bear. Here at last was an end to pretence. For Anne, a chance to adopt so naturally the predominant, masculine role, protective and caring of a woman. For Eugene, the sheer delight of being treated not as the hardened master of Kung Fu, a fine example of male strength and power, but as a vulnerable woman, hungry for the loving attentions of a man.

They stood for the most part in silence, both at peace, yet neither daring to confide too much too soon. For now, it was enough to adopt their natural roles with one another; unnecessary at this stage to voice their respective insights into the other's true sexuality.

Eugene, anxious that this snatch of happiness should not disappear, looked for reassurance that Anne felt the same as he did.

'I asked her if we'd see one another again. To my relief, she said "yes", straightaway. I daren't think what I'd have done if she'd said no.'

'But I had to know more – what about the person she was living with, her husband? She said "He's not my husband, at least I don't feel as though he is." It was more than I'd dared to hope for.'

Eventually, reluctantly, it was time to go and as the mood changed, Eugene felt the old confusions return.

'I started to panic. What was I doing here like this? I thought I must be going mad, it was silly, behaving like a soft woman. Who was I kidding? It was an illusion. Eugene Lung began to take over and I felt safe again. But within I knew that what we'd just experienced together was the real me; it was no good trying to pretend otherwise, not anymore.'

By the time they met again at the following week's class, both were in a state of nervous anticipation, of scarcely concealed excitement. For Anne it seemed a logical reaction.

'When you're trapped in the wrong body, it's as if your emotions stop developing, never reach their full adult level. The man inside me was like a young adolescent boy experiencing the thrill of the chase, of love for the first time. So I got the tingles, the thrills, I just couldn't help myself.'

Liz sensed that something was up.

'It was written all over Anne's face the moment she came in, I'd never seen her looking so pleased. She told me she'd asked Eugene out and that they'd been for a meal and now she was thinking of taking him to Stratford, to the theatre or the pictures. I must say I was surprised. I'm sure I knew that she wasn't really happy with Andrew, though she'd never said as much. But if Eugene was going to chat anyone up I'd have thought it would've been Nita – she was little and blonde and attractive. Anne was very nice and certainly not plain – she had attractive long hair and a pleasant face – but I suppose I just never expected it of her.'

It aroused interest and some jealousy among the other girls too.

'A lot of them came up to me in the changing room, half-joking really, but they said "What's this we hear then? How come he's going out with you and not one of us?" I had to smile myself. If only they knew Eugene as I felt I did, had seen him respond to me the way he did that night.'

The gentle teasing and gossip hardly seemed to matter much – Anne had always been one to go her own way and Eugene, as teacher was beyond reproach.

So the odd courtship continued, the two meeting whenever they could snatch a few hours away from the everyday world, and once alone together each automatically assuming the opposite role, Anne the man, Eugene his lady.

Yet still neither could or would admit to the other what was happening. As if by mutual and silent consent they responded to the other, without need of explanation, of any deeper interpretation than that both preferred to act and be treated as members of the opposite sex.

Caught up in the strength of her feelings for Eugene, Anne had temporarily put aside the problem of her marriage and of Andrew's horrifying involvement with the occult. Despite the risk of discovery, she saw no apparent harm in letting him come to class for an "open evening", and for what promised to be an impressive demonstration by the Lung brothers. Andrew, totally unaware of his wife's infatuation, was curious to meet this Master Sifu of whom he had heard so much, both as an exponent of Kung Fu and as a spiritual figurehead.

It was an odd gesture, but he arrived at the hall bearing a small Chinese cabbage fresh picked from his garden. It was a gift for Eugene who, already wary and on the defensive, received his present with suspicious ill-grace.

'To me it seemed more like a portent of bad, of evil. I could sense that this man meant me harm and that somehow this cabbage was a stupid symbol. He'd intended it as a threat to try and influence me to do something, but just what that was I couldn't see.'

Jealousy had begun to consume Eugene.

'I felt overwhelmed to think that Anne should be married to this man. I wanted to scream out "No! she's mine, keep away from her" – or more to the point, "keep away from *him*", from the man I'm beginning to love!'

These all seemed crazy notions in what was soon to become a crazy situation. Crazy to the onlooker, but nothing short of terrifying to those involved. For it seemed obvious to Anne that her husband saw in Eugene his long-awaited spiritual adviser. True to the *Tales of Power*, Andrew had been searching for someone to guide him onto the path to full acceptance by the force itself. Now he was convinced that Eugene was the very person, and that through him the spirit would be unleashed. Whatever the truth of the matter, it presented a tangled web which Anne confronted with a mounting anger.

'I watched Andrew glaring at Eugene and I felt not so much afraid of what might happen, of what he might do next, but furious to think that this evil thing had come unbidden to influence us all so profoundly – and we seemed helpless to do anything about it.'

She felt all her potential happiness with Eugene evaporating into confusion. She had to get away, to be alone, take a breather and review her future.

It was a time for decisions to be made, decisions which she could only make for herself; and so packing her bicycle she set off to ride south to Devon, hoping, along the way, to find the answers to several important questions.

'I'd never been off on my own before, but I was so worried and preoccupied about what to do for the best that I never gave it a second thought. No one else could give me advice, it was something I had to work out for myself, I was tired of prevaricating.'

Her head was a jumble of thoughts and emotions, hopelessly confused.

'Just about everything was mixed up. Exactly what was I? That was the crux of it all. I wasn't a lesbian, that I knew now to be true. Yet I was attracted to women – but now here I was acting strangely with Eugene, and frankly loving it – and at the same time I was still married to Andrew.

'What was I going to do? Was I going to carry on living with him or was I attracted to becoming something other than a wife? I'd got no money, we were always permanently broke, so if I left him, where would I live?'

It was a ruthless self-examination and one Anne had studiously avoided until now. But if she was to pursue the best opportunity that had ever presented itself in her life, then this agonizing was vital.

But the trip she planned was intended as something of a holiday too – her first break since that disastrous episode in Wales – and she needed something to read. Again, her choice was random – Kate Millett, an authoress she knew, seemed appealing – and she picked the first book that fell out of the shelf, *Flying*. It came out to be read at every stop, Anne gripped by the tale of a bisexual woman, her struggle to realize her identity and her experiences of living with her Japanese lover. Given Anne's own predicament and her affection for Eugene, ostensibly from China, it all seemed relevant. Fact and fiction, reality and pretence had merged so often lately that they were fast becoming indistinguishable.

It was hot, hard work cycling across the expansive measure of Salisbury Plain. But the scenery was breathtaking. Anne was nearing Stonehenge, the ancient Druid ruins, the very heart of symbolism and ritualistic worship. She reached the towering circle of plinths, exhausted and glad to lie and rest for a while in the hot sun. As she ate some fruit, she chuckled to herself, considering how fitting it was to be contemplating her future in such a place. A sense of the power and pattern of fate and the ironies of life were never lost on Anne.

'As I sat there quietly I began to wonder what would happen if I turned my whole world inside out, if I faced up to the one obvious and glaring truth.

'No, I wasn't a lesbian, I wasn't even a woman – what I really was was a man!

'Suddenly it all seemed simple, I'd finally resolved all the questions I'd always been asking and never allowed myself to answer.'

All the instincts, the subconscious longings, her mixed feelings about her body fell into a tangled pattern which at last had been unravelled.

The relief at being able to erase, once and for all, the lie of her femininity was indescribable. Anything was possible, there was no point in continuing the charade or of trying to suppress the feelings that had grown familiar since she was a child. For they were natural, a part of her that was not quirky, peculiar or even queer. Now she had had the courage to allow them to develop there was to be no going back; in fact, that was the last thing she wanted.

Now she felt tired, and suddenly calm.

'It was such an obvious and natural conclusion and now I had faced up to it, all the years of trouble and longing just melted away.'

The agony which Anne was experiencing was not lost on Eugene, and he spent the time she was away in a restless fervour. He could not sleep and he lay in bed for hours tossing violently, praying to the God in whom he had always believed.

He knew nothing of Andrew's inescapable involvement with strange and dubious forces, yet his own psychic sensibilities warned him that something was seriously wrong.

'I recognized that he was evil and I was terrified that he'd use it to influence Anne into never coming back to me, but instead to carry on with him in some sort of bisexual limbo. It made me crazy, I felt so mad that there was nothing I could do – I couldn't go and find her, I had no idea where she'd gone. To imagine being without her was unbearable.'

For those who knew him it was a frightening time. Eugene was like a caged animal, his aggression turned on anyone and anything that dared to get in his way.

'Thank God for the punchball! If I hadn't had that to kick out at I'd most likely have done someone a serious injury. I'd never felt so strange, so wild before.'

Eventually and mainly through sheer exhaustion the panic subsided and Eugene reverted to the best way he knew of regaining his equilibrium – meditation. Shut in his room in the rambling, decaying house that was home, he drew for strength not just on Buddha but on God.

His love, the one person who knew and wanted him for what he really was, was in danger, was at a crossroads in her life. Please God, she must choose the right road, she must come back to him, so protect her God, from the wicked forces he knew were all around her – please, if he had a God, He had helped him before, so please help him now.

So ran the desperate pleas Eugene repeated countless times

both day and night. Melodramatic cries for help maybe, but as it turned out, fully justified.

In part his prayers were answered. Anne returned home, by all accounts in one piece and her mind made up. She knew now that she could not continue as Andrew's wife, that this time, whatever else she did, she would have to leave him. She still had no clear picture of what would follow, of where she would go.

'I thought to myself that if I didn't end up somewhere on my own I could always find myself a woman to live with!'

The possibility of that woman being Eugene was something she had not even contemplated.

That night she told Andrew that their marriage was over. There was little bitterness or animosity, but her husband was upset.

'Whatever else was going on I did still care about her. I tried to hammer into her that she shouldn't leave me, but it seemed that she'd really made up her mind this time.'

The talk continued on a somewhat strained but highly civilized vein, of money settlements and division of property. It was agreed that Anne should stay until she could find somewhere to set up home, preferably on her own.

They had no savings, the extension to the house was only half finished, and by rights half of all they possessed was Anne's. The only eventual solution seemed to be a second mortgage, of two thousand pounds, on paper to pay for the building work, in fact to finance Anne's independence, so enabling Andrew to keep the house.

It was a blatant deception and flouting of the law, but there seemed no option if things were to be settled quickly. Finishing off the alterations to render the place saleable could take months given their recurring cash flow problem.

Even so, the arrangements were to take time, and while her marriage staggered to its conclusion, Anne continued to find solace with Eugene. She had told no one, not even him, of the real reason behind her decision to leave home; but she did confide her worst fears for Andrew.

Eugene was afraid for her more than ever.

'If there was this evil, then we could expect trouble and we would have to fight it together.'

They began to meet for meditation, sitting quietly together

in Eugene's room. They talked about faith, but it was no use. Religion was one source of help Anne firmly rejected. She was an atheist and did not believe she could rely on anyone other than herself to find a solution to her problem, certainly not some god. Still Eugene persisted; his faith was the only way he knew to counter what he and Anne were up against, for he was convinced that Andrew would retaliate, would not be prepared to let his wife go that easily. He was to be proven right, but his anticipated clash with Andrew turned out to be more a battle of wits between the two of them than a direct threat to Anne. Since the *Tales of Power* had been introduced unwittingly into their lives, the couple had become more and more competitive, spending most of their time scoring points off one another, taking delight in outachieving each other. Now Anne had realized her own masculinity the reasons for this became clearer, for all the time theirs had been a conflict of men, not of husband and wife. Now Anne felt reassured, free of interference, confident even, but Eugene refused to be other than pessimistic.

From their very first meeting, the premonition of evil he had seen in Andrew had been mutual. To Andrew, Master Sifu was not just a spiritual adviser, he was a corrupt being. For both men it was a challenge as Andrew duly recognized.

'I realized he was possessed, we each saw it in the other. But I felt this desire to dominate, to take control. That was how it'd been with Anne, I wasn't under her thumb anymore and she resented that, the more forceful I became the more it frightened her.'

By now things were getting out of hand, and even Andrew felt appalled when he paused, which was not often, in his almost maniacal pursuit of power. He needed help if his subjugation was not to prove final.

Anne turned to Eugene. It was an absurd notion, to imagine that the person who was by all accounts her boyfriend should want to intervene to save the man who remained, in name at least, her husband. Still, life could hardly have been stranger than it was at that moment and while Anne was clearly out of her depth in the world of spiritualism, Eugene was, by reputation, something of an expert.

In any case, they were so drawn to each other, so close, that Eugene seemed the best person to turn to.

Anne and Eugene sat in a pub one evening after class, and

109

agreed that Andrew had to be faced if the evil he was tangled up in was not going to consume them all. There would have to be a confrontation, Eugene and he would have to meet.

Sedate, conservative Solihull could not have had the vaguest notion of the bizarre scene that was acted out in the Biddulphs' living room that Thursday night – the shock would have brought the town to its knees!

Anne, seated in an armchair, was to witness a confrontation none of them would ever forget. Andrew, facing Eugene, was scowling – angry, upset and growing more so.

Eugene tried to radiate reassurance; he knew there was something dreadfully wrong, but he was there to help. Andrew was mistrustful, feeling usurped in his own home. Yet in desperation he admitted his own fear. 'It's gone from me now, but it'll be back!'

It was a start, and Eugene seized it. Drawing on his considerable sense of the theatrical, he yelled back:

'In the name of Jesus Christ, you must find God if you're to be saved!' It was theatre, right enough, yet the essence of what he said was no blasphemy but spoken from the heart. Sifu Lung may have strayed a long way from Irish Catholicism, but his personal faith remained intact. Incredibly, his shock tactics seemed to work. For Andrew, gaunt, palefaced, the ardent disbeliever, fell on his knees begging God's forgiveness. As he did so, Eugene felt an intangible presence leave the man bent double at his feet and again he called on Andrew in the name of the Saviour, to come to his senses, to reject the force commanding his mind.

Anne was upset, feeling helpless to intervene and hearing Eugene call on God so willingly angered her beyond measure.

All her life she had had an unspoken quarrel with God over her identity, her birth into what had proved to be the wrong body. Both she and Andrew had firmly rejected religion and it seemed outrageous to maintain that any god could help them now. For what seemed like hours, they watched as Andrew wrestled helplessly with his mind and with the parasitical power that had turned him from a good-natured, kindly man into a fountain of evil.

In an almost delirious state, Andrew looked at Eugene. It was incredible, but he was certain that what he saw before him was not a man, but a woman sitting and passing judgement. He

110

could see her come and go, drifting into the depths of Eugene's eyes. Despite the terrible strain of concentration, when Andrew told of what he saw, Eugene could not help but feel elated, certain as he was that what Andrew had glimpsed was the woman he kept hidden within himself, the woman he knew to be his true spirit. It was as though Andrew's heightened perceptions had enabled him to reach beyond the outer Eugene in his search for a guide and mentor.

'Despite all our differences I felt that at that moment Andrew actually understood me, almost as though he felt a love for this woman whom he saw as his spiritual adviser come to bring him enlightenment. It sounded bizarre, but I was in tune with him, somehow I knew what he meant, I was in total sympathy.'

Only Anne remained on a more rational plane, frustrated by her inability to reach the level of metaphysical understanding enjoyed by the other two.

Eugene needed no convincing that it was God Himself who controlled the events of that night, who had successfully engineered the clash between Andrew and himself, so that Andrew could find solace in His indulgence.

It had been a tumultuous experience for them all, but once it was over Andrew conceded that it had left him feeling calmed and considerably reassured.

Now that it had passed, there seemed little point in prolonging the evening with a pretence of hospitality. Andrew needed more than anything to sleep, but he promised to sit up and wait while Anne drove Eugene home. If he then realized his wife's attachment to the curious little Oriental, he made no mention of it, for nothing seemed more remote; after his recent ordeal all other considerations seemed to pale into insignificance.

For once, Anne and Eugene had little to say to each other, as though both found the past hours too disconcerting to provoke conversation. Anne drove automatically, her mind pitching from worry over Andrew to anger that something vile and intangible had come uninvited into their home and, she was certain, had settled there. Parking the car in the drive on her return home, she went inside. Andrew had gone to bed; the house was in pitch darkness and imbued with an unmistakably eerie atmosphere given what had just taken place.

The lightswitch was across the sitting room and feeling fraught and annoyed Anne walked tentatively towards it.

Someone or something was sitting by the fireside in Andrew's chair; it must be him, she could sense his presence. Jumpy in the dark, she realized her mind was playing tricks, Andrew was upstairs, the whole thing was ridiculous, nothing more than a nervous reaction.

She did not panic, being more angry than afraid. She was certain the force had returned, she could feel it filling the room.

Exasperated, she went to the kitchen, hoping to find something which might bring her thoughts back to the real world. Pretend to be busy; pretend all is well, she was telling herself; quite suddenly, she noticed she was getting together food and frying pan, cooking bacon, cracking eggs.

All of a sudden she was hungry, ravenous; at the same time, she couldn't help feeling that there was something sinister behind her subconscious efforts to prepare a meal.

Nevertheless, the meal was a comfort, satisfying her sudden hunger. Afterwards she sat on the settee, reliving the strange evening in her mind's eye, feeling numbed by the experience – it all seemed so outrageous now, though she felt it had been worthwhile for Andrew's sake.

How could life have become so twisted and convoluted? What had she done, unwittingly or otherwise, to deserve this? As if her physical malformity was not more than enough to bear, now there some kind of malevolent spirit that she did not understand that had invaded her life. She closed her eyes, felt old and weary, unable to influence her future. Andrew chose that moment to stumble downstairs, disturbed by the clatter in the kitchen. He slumped in his armchair, viewing his wife with some derision; she for her part was horrified. The venomous presence had indeed remained to haunt them; she could see it now, engulfing the man she had once loved and who, because of some unshakeable mantle of evil, had been altered beyond recognition.

She felt furious with this man, once her husband, who now seemed alert and once again hostile. The more she challenged him, the more Andrew denied that he was possessed, so that despite her better judgement – urging her to quit, to get out fast – she found herself face to face with a being which, try as she might, she could not recognize or understand.

The conflict which had enveloped every part of their relationship for months was reaching a kind of climax. How much of it was self-willed, to do with their personal antagonisms, and how much pure surrealism was hard to judge, but even Anne's innate cynicism could not shake her conviction that supernatural influences were indeed at work.

By three-thirty the tension was unbearable. Anne's arms and shoulders shook with an internal force she had not known she possessed, the heavy burdensome feeling she had first experienced in the Pennines was with her again. As if responding to the weird mood, the three cats, who had at first revelled in this unexpected early morning company, began howling desperately, stalking the room as if in search of prey. As the atmosphere worsened they dashed from the room in blatant terror.

The moment seemed poisonous, full of danger, and for her own safety Anne knew she must create a barrier between it and her. Already she felt the antagonism between the demoniacal spirit sitting parasitically on Andrew and her own internal life force, which sprung to her defence so forcibly now, her every nerve on edge, her body taut as if willing the waves of power between them to subside.

Acting purely on instinct she began waving her hands in vague, sweeping patterns, as if the motions would somehow subdue the power, would boomerang it back to Andrew and maybe beyond him and out of their lives. Anne was clutching at straws, but as she felt her own determination well up so she began to utter weird grunts and cries, as if by so doing she could somehow mesmerize the inhuman opposition into submission.

So they sat, a curiously pitiful tableau, the couple, who had once been so close, alienated as they had never imagined possible. For hours Anne kept up the momentum, willing with all her might that the spirit would leave them once and for all.

Finally it did, in the early dawn, when both Anne and Andrew became gradually aware that an intolerable pressure was lifting.

'I felt it leave him, but there was nothing to see, he just sat there, staring at me as if to say, it's no good girl, you've won. I knew he was weak, but already he was beginning to look better, I couldn't feel the evil anymore.'

Andrew came towards her on his knees; the horror had been a shared experience which was to draw them momentarily closer than they had been for some considerable time. Anne cradled him in her arms, rocking their bodies in comfortable unison as Andrew confessed to the dreadful ambitions the spirit had planted in his twisted mind.

He had wanted to kill Anne, he had even planned how to do it during the months that the power sat in harness on his shoulder. Now he felt empty, unwhole, a human shell without a soul. It was a pitiful sight, the despair and sheer exhaustion obvious in every limb. A weariness neither had known before made it impossible to think of moving, or of releasing their embrace. Even now Anne found it difficult to feel at peace – for yet another infinitely alarming worry had filled her thought. During the night she was now convinced that she had witnessed the work of evil, in all probability of the Devil himself. That being so, then it followed that in recognizing and combating evil she had to acknowledge the good force which had undoubtedly made that possible, namely God. For a confirmed atheist it was a mighty admission to allow and the beginning of a tussle with the Christian faith that continues to this day.

For the moment her mind was so blitzed with the bizarre turn of events, so preoccupied with the immediate future, that she could barely contemplate any further disruption. Torpidly she shuffled to the kitchen, made tea and went thankfully to bed. It was the first time in her life that she had stayed up all night, and she sincerely hoped that it was the last.

After two hours' heavy sleep she awoke in a cold sweat, remembering only too clearly what had gone before. There was no sign of Andrew, presumably he had somehow summoned the energy to stagger to work.

Several miles away in Handsworth, Eugene had spent the night pacing the floor, furious with himself for leaving Anne to cope alone, realizing as he did the inevitability of Andrew's force returning, and once challenged, proving more insistent than before. As daylight appeared he began to pray fervently for Anne to come to him; he could visualize all too clearly what had taken place: he knew that Andrew had left – just as certainly as he knew that he would return, and that the next time there would be no respite for Anne.

For a while Anne sat in bed thinking over her next move. She had no intention of staying in the cottage a moment longer than was necessary; all her notions of its unfriendliness had been proven now and she was not anxious to prolong the agony. Nor was she happy to involve her parents in such an inexplicable affair, for if she sought refuge with them Andrew was bound to follow, bringing with him, perhaps, the evil spirit that was stalking him. She was sincerely frightened for her parents' safety, loving them too deeply to let them suffer on her behalf.

Her only alternative was to go to Eugene. True, her original plan on leaving Andrew was to set up home alone, or, as she had half-joked to herself, with another woman.

Yet it was Eugene to whom she was irresistibly drawn, Eugene who seemed to understand as no other her need to act as a man, and who freely allowed her to do so when she was with him. If nothing else, she needed to share rationally with him the experiences of that strange night, to find refuge and friendship with the only other person to have shared the incredible experience. She was too tired and drained emotionally to face a barrage of questions at work. For once her clients would have to take care of themselves.

She took the now familiar route across town to Handsworth, somewhat surprised to find life outside her house continuing as normal. Somehow she had expected the entire world to have been changed, for better or worse she wasn't sure, by the episode that only Andrew, Eugene and she had actually experienced.

As she sat in the traffic, she noticed a cyclist pedalling towards her. He passed by, heading in the direction she had just come from and she could have sworn that it was Andrew. She was never able to confirm that it had indeed been him, but for Anne the look on the face of the man she maintains was her husband, has remained unforgettable.

'It was the intense look I had seen on him all night; a look of venomous hatred and sinister intent that was just hideous to see. I really believed that I had had a near miss and that Andrew had purposely tricked me by going to work. Now he was heading home again, expecting to find me and catch me unawares. If there was a God after all, then he must've had me at heart to make me leave when I did'.

Perhaps the strain was telling, her imagination working overtime, but it all helped to justify her final departure.

12

Having sensed what Anne had been going through at the cottage since his departure, Eugene was pleased to see her at his doorstep and welcomed her warmly. He had "witnessed" the scenes so vividly in his imagination there was hardly any point in asking Anne what had happened and, by the look of her, an inquisition was the last thing she needed. If she had been amazed by his own actions and by the unexpected strength of his religious fervour, then there would be time enough to discuss that later. Eugene's soul was alive with joy and anticipation at the thought that his lover had come to him, not simply for consolation, but perhaps to stay.

For the remainder of that grey November day the two of them sat quietly together, thankful beyond measure that they had found one another. By the evening both knew that there was no question of Anne ever returning to her home or to her marriage, and the next morning Anne made up her mind to stay. Eugene broke the news to his long-suffering family that, if it was all right with them, his married girlfriend was moving in.

May and Eugene Senior had been so buffeted, over the years, by their eldest son's colourful lifestyle that they were able to take this latest turn of events in their stride. They had already grown used to his make-believe *alter ego*, Lung. That he should take up with a woman friend and want her to move in was a novel twist in Eugene Junior's unconventional behaviour, but if she made their son happy then they would generously welcome Anne into their home.

His father took Eugene to one side; knowing as he did of his son's childhood fantasies, his problems with women in the past, he needed to be certain that this was really what Eugene wanted, to set up home with a woman.

'I had no trouble reassuring him that I was absolutely certain of what I was doing. I felt more sure than I dared to disclose, because what Dad and no one else realized was that Anne was the one person with whom I could really be myself and that meant being a woman!'

If Anne was to move in she needed to collect some clothes, and a few belongings, which meant returning to the cottage. They decided to go together, fearing repercussions, and as they turned into the driveway they immediately sensed the leaden, moribund atmosphere that pervaded the place. Inside the cottage things were no better; the cats were distraught, and leaving them behind was Anne's one regret.

One journey proved not to be enough; their car was not exactly a limousine and in their haste to put the bleak cottage behind them, Anne overlooked a number of things. Next day they made a return trip; but this time, as Anne packed a few forgotten belongings, Andrew showed up. He attempted pleasantries, seemingly unaware that a sinister and evil mien betrayed his true feelings.

Eugene felt uncomfortable, an intruder into what seemed a purely private moment between husband and estranged wife. He wanted to leave but was reluctant to do so, concerned that Anne might not be able to cope with the situation without moral support. At the same time, though, he sensed that Andrew was afraid of her.

As soon as Andrew realized what was happening, that his wife was finally carrying out her threat to leave him, he became sullen and curt. It was clear that her affections lay with Eugene, and Andrew suddenly felt very lonely and distraught. It was an awkward yet portentous moment for all three of them.

They had taken the first step. Anne had made her decision, they had dealt with Andrew, and now the time had come to start building a new life for themselves, to discover one another, not surreptitiously during stolen rendezvous behind Andrew's back, but through an open and adult heterosexual relationship.

That second night they slept in one another's arms, experiencing a closeness and a unity that neither had felt with anyone else ever before. They could not help feeling that a new and exciting chapter in their lives was opening.

To the outside world they must have appeared an oddly

matched couple; Anne was taller than Eugene, of firmer build, unmistakably female despite her customary trousers, while Eugene's small, wiry frame was usually adorned in the oriental fashions he loved so much, flamboyant in comparison with his partner. Yet to see them together, no one could have doubted their great affection for one another; they drew the strength from their relationship to be quite demonstrative in public, holding hands and embracing without the slightest embarrassment.

An odd looking pair, perhaps, but one which most people thought conventional and congenial company. No one would have guessed at the curious and distinctly unorthodox approach they adopted to their physical relationship. Just as they had begun their courtship with complete sexual honesty, so they were to continue, to their mutual and growing satisfaction.

Eugene had felt somewhat reticent at first, but his confidence in Anne grew quickly and he soon learned that there was nothing to fear in allowing their relationship to become intimate. Instinctively they reversed roles during sex, and in so doing experienced the joys of physical love for the first time.

Anne and Eugene found it easier to follow their sexual instincts than to discuss them, but privately they both felt that helping each other to overcome the hurdle of intercourse had cemented their relationship and brought the prospect of a fulfilling life closer. Not that sexual truth was by any stretch of the imagination the total answer. Sex was important but could always have been coped with somehow. The more fundamental problem was gender. Yet they still felt the need to tread carefully, for the ideas and emotions buzzing through their minds and hearts were wild, audacious, controversial; too new to be rushed, but too exciting to be ignored.

It was not until they had been lovers for some weeks that Eugene could voice the knowledge that he had held close since their very first encounter. Only then did he feel secure enough in their relationship to broach the unmentionable. Could Anne, did she like women?

'She said of course she did, she was fond of them, in fact she found them very fascinating.'

From that point Eugene found it surprisingly easy to confide the secret which had burdened him all his life. She must try to understand, he was a woman, deep within himself that was what he was.

Anne could hardly contain herself: here was confirmation of her own intuitive understanding of Eugene; of the femininity she had recognized and reacted to so strongly in the time they had spent together. At the same time, in so bravely declaring himself, Eugene had confirmed what she had always felt to be true of herself. She very eagerly assured him that she had felt from the start that he was indeed a female.

After that, it was a much smaller step than Anne had imagined to admit that if Eugene believed himself to be a woman, she was no less a man – and if he had lived a lie all his life, then so had she. These were momentous confessions to make to oneself, let alone to another person, and both of them experienced a sense of immense relief almost as soon as the words were uttered.

Confession *was* good for the soul, but it did little to improve their way of life beyond the bedroom, certainly not beyond their own front door. But it did provide their relationship with a solid foundation of trust and understanding, a closeness of heart and spirit which few couples manage to attain.

It gave Eugene a sense of security that he had not known before. Being honest with himself, able to admit the truth and share the consequences with a sympathetic person, was an exhilarating release.

His new-found peace of mind, combined with the continued physical rigours of his beloved Kung Fu, served as an antidote to the confusion and despondency he had suffered for well over twenty years, and it was with renewed enthusiasm that he now threw himself into his work. He found it less of an ordeal to watch the women in his class now that he knew his secret was shared and he demonstrated a fresh vigour and stridency in his martial arts tutorials.

Of course there was the family to face. Eugene wanted to get to know the Johnsons and, hopefully, be accepted by them. True to form, Anne had kept her parents in ignorance about her rocky marriage and if they had sensed that all was not well, then they had not broached the matter with her. She was afraid of what their reaction might be; they were genuinely fond of their son-in-law and Anne knew that she would never be able to convince them that he was impossible to live with, let alone a man possessed by the devil – they would think Anne was crazy!

She also knew that it would be extremely difficult to present the truth about the way her relationship with Eugene was developing to her parents. It was bad enough that she was conducting what they would see as an adulterous affair – they were bound to disapprove. But to try to make them understand that she believed herself to be a man. . .

To their credit, the Johnsons tried hard to accept their youngest's change of fortune and of partner with something approaching equanimity, and they insisted on the couple continuing the weekly ritual visit for tea or Sunday lunch as if nothing untoward had happened. Somehow their approval was vital to Anne for her peace of mind, for the idea that she might be causing them anxiety distressed her.

Eugene never felt comfortable during his visits to the Johnsons, but then family tea parties were not something with which he was exactly familiar. Still, their visits encouraged the Johnson family to accept them slowly as a couple.

In contrast, Anne met little resistance from the Browns. Eugene's family took to her from the beginning; May was delighted to have another woman around the house, even if the newcomer did not conform to her image of the domesticated female.

13

It was during Anne and Eugene's first Christmas together that the need to explore their emotional desires and inclinations further came to the fore. They no longer found it enough simply to swop roles during lovemaking, nor for Anne to act as the dominant figure to whom Eugene acquiesced in day-to-day matters. They both felt the urgent need to take whatever steps were necessary to shed their false genders and reveal their true selves.

With the blossoming of their romance, Eugene had begun to take greater trouble over his personal grooming, not simply out of deference to his mistress, but because the more she treated him as a woman, the more he felt the need to act like one. He had let his hair grow long, was even considering having it permed. On Christmas morning Anne watched as he dressed himself.

'Suddenly she said she'd love to see me as a female, not just acting like one, but dressed like one too.'

Despite his own yearnings, Eugene felt mildly embarrassed, for while he had frequently dressed as a woman before, he had never revealed himself in women's clothes to anyone apart from his mother. Now he was worried that Anne would be disappointed in his feminine guise, that the ideal of Eugene that she carried in her imagination was way beyond what was really possible.

Anne was insistent, and eventually, after some clever cajoling, persuaded Eugene to put on a skirt which she had hardly ever felt inclined to wear herself. He stood before her, no parody of womanhood, for despite the firm muscular frame, and the male complexion, there was an intangible naturalness in his demeanour and the way he carried himself that made the clothing fit unashamedly well. The moment wasn't silly or sordid; Eugene's was neither the act of a clown dressing up for a lark nor that of a transvestite. The purpose of "cross-dressing" was not to raise a cheap thrill. Eugene did not experience any sexual gratification from knowing that a male organ was hidden underneath the skirt. Instead he felt a profound relief at finally being able to give expression to his instincts and a deep-rooted empathy with womanhood. Nothing he had done so far in his life seemed as natural as this moment, and suddenly the weight of perpetuating the charade of his maleness was lifted.

Anne's amazement at the success of his physical tranformation was proof, if any was needed, that the answer to Eugene's predicament lay in finding some way to make the change permanent.

'She was staring at me. She said she couldn't believe it, and she went on and on, telling me how much she liked me, how I was beautiful, she hadn't realized just how beautiful before. I felt marvellous – apart from feeling right dressed like that, no one had ever told me I was beautiful before.'

It was an exciting and momentous development in their relationship, an experience which Eugene was to repeat frequently when they were alone; but it caused Anne intolerable anguish. Now that the vision of Eugene as a woman had been given form, she longed to love that woman in a way which was natural and conformed to her and society's sense of propriety.

It was an impossible hope, as unattainable as sprouting wings and being able to fly. She resented the necessity of continually taking the birth pill and was at her most depressed whenever she started to menstruate, a bodily function she considered a biological betrayal of her manhood.

Bemoaning her inability to consummate her love for Eugene correctly and properly, Anne began to nurse a cancerous frustration. She was trapped, caged by the limbs, torso and organs which branded her so firmly as a woman, while her outlook, senses and psyche were so adamantly male. The promise of their life together was tempered by the burden of their ambiguous emotional existence, yet through it all their conviction never wavered.

With the New Year came the chance of a fresh start: Anne's mortgage money meant that they could afford the deposit on a home of their own. By now their fragile bond had survived for several months, and was showing all the signs of strengthening into a permanent relationship. Accordingly, the couple duly made an investment in a small Victorian villa house, set in a terraced row, well maintained for its age. Their new neighbourhood was Stetchford, conveniently close to the Browns and to Anne's work. It was the first time Eugene had anywhere he could call his own; he had always lived together with his family wherever they had made their home, and it was a refreshing challenge to be able to break out. In those early days, Anne and Eugene's possessions were few – a mattress on the floor was their bed, makeshift items of furniture – but Anne set about decorating with a vengeance and turning their meagre personal belongings into a presentable and welcoming home.

They were rarely short of visitors, relatives and friends from work and the Kung Fu classes were all frequent visitors.

All this time the Martial Arts School was flourishing, Eugene's brother Michael proving a highly competent tutor. He was, if anything, better suited to the rigours of teaching, being less of a taskmaster than Eugene and thus considered more approachable by his disciples.

Tim Ward was well pleased with the way his faith in the Lungs was being rewarded, and if they clashed over the question of money more and more regularly, their pay negotiations were conducted in fairly amicable manner. The brothers were often called upon to perform at fetes and charity shows and Anne became a regular spectator in what were often huge crowds. Their speciality act was a spectacular set of Wu Shu, a weird and wonderful form of Chinese gymnastics, performed to music and demanding extraordinary skill. It inevitably brought the house down.

As a side line Tim encouraged Eugene to employ his paranormal abilities in compiling horoscopes, based on the well proven Chai Ching principle, which would hopefully predict changes of fortune. It was purely a business venture with the horoscopes being sold and published in various martial arts magazines, more on good faith than credibility. But what began as something of a stunt proved surprisingly accurate. Eugene was to write horoscopes on a regular basis until he felt himself under-valued, demanded and was refused better payment and eventually gave it up.

With all these preoccupations it was easy to let Andrew

Biddulph slip unhappily into the past, but various loose ends of the marriage still had to be tied up and they had, reluctantly, to meet again.

Once more it was to be a traumatic confrontation, for immediately Andrew arrived, it was as if their home was filled by the demonic, oppressive atmosphere they had previously encountered at the cottage. As before, the clash of spirits was violent and frightening, for both Eugene and Andrew were determined to win this time; but now Andrew himself was plainly scared.

'I knew now that I was demon possessed, there were no two ways about it. When I clashed with Eugene it was as if I was going mad, there seemed to be no escape. On the one hand I had this terrifying force controlling everything that I did, and on the other there was the spirit I could see in Eugene, which to me was equally wicked.'

Once again Eugene had recourse to God, without whom he maintained to Anne, there was no hope. This time and with considerable melodrama, he pulled from his pocket a tiny crucifix which, holding before him, he pointed long and hard at a cowering Andrew.

'He shouted at me that I was the reincarnation of Judas, that I must look to God to forgive me. I was completely incoherent, I'm convinced he was trying to send me out of my mind.' It was an incredible confrontation between the two, but one for which Andrew was later to be grateful. For thanks to Eugene the unrelenting torture he had suffered was about to end in a weird storybook fashion that somehow epitomized the whole bizarre episode.

So distraught had he become by the sight of the crucifix, which lured him like a magic charm, that running from the house he drove wildly to the one place where he knew he would find sanctuary, the local oratory.

It was indeed the reaction of a man insane, but by now Andrew knew the truth of it and while he had never acknowledged religion in any context, it was in desperation that he now turned to the priest for help.

'I begged him to give me a crucifix and he gave me one and told me to go to the chapel. I couldn't even reply I was so incoherent, but he didn't seem to want any explanation.'

Andrew had never prayed in his life, he did not know how. 'I just shouted out "God if you're there, forgive me." It was a desperate little cry, but it was all I could think of and I just kept on shouting it out loud.'

It was sufficient, for his entire body, bloated with the voices and visions, the hallucinations he had come to live with, shook before falling limp; the evil had finally been expelled. For Andrew it was a momentous event that was to radically change his life; from then on he was to become a regular worshipper at the Elim Church, to study the Bible so that he knew it by heart and eventually to become a member of the Pentecostal church. He knew he had been saved and for that everyone was thankful.

14

The arrival of Emma Johnson Lung as she was to be duly named and registered, did indeed mark a new beginning for Anne and Eugene. Part one of the plan had been successful and if it left the new parents emotionally drained, it also brought them an indescribable relief that it was over. For Anne there were several days' recuperation from her operation. It proved to be a busy time, for now that the baby had actually arrived, the Johnsons as well as the Browns were more than eager to be part of the glad event. The new grandparents visited the hospital regularly; May Brown particularly thrilled to have a girl in the family at last, the Johnsons equally delighted that Anne had finally got round to becoming a mother. Even Andrew telephoned the ward, amazed at his estranged wife's conformity in having a child after the years of adamant refusal even to contemplate such a thing. He had finally left the horrors of possession behind him and in a complete conversion to religion was an ardent member of the Pentecostal church and a confirmed Christian. He had even set about becoming a pastor and a missionary. For the moment, though, he wanted Anne back. 'He told me that leaving him, living with Eugene and having the baby, all that was forgiven. Now all he wanted was for me to go back, he would even look after my child if I did. He literally pleaded with me to give up Eugene, but I'm afraid all that I could feel was pity. To me it seemed obvious that he was under pressure from the church not to get divorced and he was hoping against hope that we could make a go of it together.'

That may well have been the case, but for Anne there was no question of returning to her old life. She remained fond of

Andrew, even anxious for his well-being, but now she loved Eugene and together they were about to take on the world.

Apart from the visitors, the nursing staff were intent on teaching all the novice mothers the rudiments of caring for their new offspring. Bathing and feeding, developing the maternal bond by holding and caressing their young, all were firmly encouraged during those first few days.

For most, these were moments to cherish, but while Anne felt an undoubted love for this little creature who was somehow her daughter, she had absolutely no desire to emulate motherhood; for a start, Emma was to be bottle-fed, despite the current vogue for breastfeeding.

No one was ever more glad to see the back of a maternity ward than Anne. It had been the most gruelling experience of her life, confirming her worst expectations; never again would she subject herself to the wretched bonds of womanhood. She knew she was a man and from now on was determined to act and live accordingly.

Once they arrived home, life for the new family took on a peculiarity all of its own. There was nothing unusual in the constant demands Emma made on her parents; what most people would have found difficult to understand was the way in which they coped.

For it was Eugene who naturally took over as Emma's mother while Anne gave the love and support expected of the good family man. It was the way both had always wanted it to be and Eugene could now revel in the maternal joys of which he had so long been denied. He took to the never ending chores of washing and feeding as if in the manner born, for so he truly was. He never tired of holding and playing with the baby daughter who in a curious way, now that the pregnancy and birth were over, had brought him a certain measure of fulfilment. Among the number of relatives and friends who came to inspect the new arrival, Liz was one of the first.

Having envisaged scenes of chaos, she was pleasantly surprised to find them fairly well organized, Emma lying happily in a baby bouncer and the room littered with nappies, tissues and creams. 'They seemed to have absolutely everything, all the baby gear imaginable. Emma was a dear little thing and to my relief Anne seemed quite okay; given the rough time she'd had with the caesarian, I thought she might've been a bit down.'

Liz could have no way of knowing the elation that her friend felt at being rid of her pregnancy; nor could she guess correctly at the reasons for Eugene's apparent absorption in the baby's welfare.

'I knew that right from the start he'd taken over all the feeding, but a short while later Anne came up to the class. She'd cut her thumb on some glass very badly and had to have it stitched, so I wondered how she was managing with Emma. She told me not to worry, Eugene did all that.'

So the pattern was set and in a gradual, cautious way their plan unfolded. It was to be beset by interminable problems, not least of which were their mounting debts. For Anne was still off work and if they were to proceed with any medical treatment, then the bills would only get worse. Even meeting the mortgage was proving impossible and there seemed nothing for it in the end but to sell the house, give up their independence and move back in with Eugene's parents. It was a prospect neither of them relished, for they had become attached to their home which, while it was hardly grand, was something of a palace in comparison to the Browns'.

Material things were becoming of less and less importance; what mattered far more was that they be allowed to go ahead with fashioning their world as they were convinced it was meant to be.

In the interim there would clearly be a need for privacy, for in their decision to deal once and for all with their problem of sexual identity, the couple laid themselves open to criticism and ill-informed opinion, much of which would be painful. Obviously, the Browns would have to know what they were intending to do if they were to live with them. For the time being, however, Anne could not face the idea of telling her own parents that she was determined to be acknowledged as a man.

The bond of affection between them was deep, yet expressed far too infrequently for her to explain the suffering she had felt all of her life; to explain that it was not some abberation on her part, but rather a natural conclusion to years of self-doubt and misinterpretation. They had no need to reproach themselves: she was their daughter, but what she thought of as her physical malformation was not of their doing and was nothing for them or anyone to feel ashamed of. So ran the explanation Anne would dearly have loved to give to her unsuspecting, loyal family. Time and time again she was simply unable to. For how could she ever expect them to understand: to live with the knowledge that their little girl was no woman at all; that since those first inklings during childhood she had felt herself to be truly male; that her marriage had failed because of her enormous self-doubts and that having Emma was a conscious sacrifice on the road to achieving her full manhood.

It all sounded too preposterous, too much a betrayal of all her family's expectations for them ever to accept without pain, and that was the last thing Anne wished to give them. If in retrospect it is fair to say that she probably underestimated their love and understanding, then it is equally fair to recognize just how great her fear was at that time.

For while the path ahead was undoubtedly the right one for both herself and for Eugene, nevertheless it was one they faced apprehensively, even fearing for their own sanity – let alone that of their relatives.

The pressure from all directions would be far too great, and if they were to see their plan through together then it was essential to devote themselves singlemindedly to achieving what they had always longed for.

Once then, that the house was sold to pay off some of their debts (in the event at something of a loss), Anne and her family sadly lost touch.

'It wasn't deliberate, but we always felt that when the time came to begin the change then we would probably have to "drop out." I was so very fond of them all that I just couldn't bear to face their reactions and all the upset. It was very hard, especially as they were growing so fond of Emma, but there seemed to be no other way.'

Indeed few people were to know of their change of address. It was as if they were withdrawing into a world of their own, one in which their very souls would be laid bare in a unique swop. For while there are far more transsexuals than is usually imagined, it is rare indeed that two of them should meet, fall in love and take one another as partners; rarer still that they should then produce a child, subsequently and deliberately turn the family unit inside out in their battle with sexual identity.

For the next three years that world was to be successfully contained within four upstairs rooms of the ramshackle house

Eugene Senior rented for a nominal sum. It was so dilapidated from the outside that few people realized it was fully occupied and for Anne and Eugene that was a distinct advantage.

Conditions were somewhat cramped with the three of them, plus the Browns and Michael Lung and his expectant wife. There were some privations; they all shared the one bathroom while in the upstairs kitchen there was no hot water; the house was fairly damp and without adequate heating. Still, it was home, there would be no questions or interference from the Browns and yet Emma would be growing up in the security of her extended family, with all the additional love her grandparents were to gladly offer.

It was against this background that they began to allow themselves greater freedom of expression than ever before. For while it had always seemed natural to adopt opposite roles and attitudes with one another, they had never made it apparent elsewhere.

Now it was vital to begin to establish themselves more distinctly to test out not so much their own ability to live the parts, but rather society's reaction to them in opposite guise. Social conditioning to roleplay was such that appearances were all important to their success. It was a shallow, superficial measure by which to judge a human being, but if Anne could capture the essence of manhood in her appearance and manner, and Eugene that of a woman, then the transformation would be so much easier.

Eugene had regularly "cross-dressed" when they were alone and it had continued to offer them both a glimpse of the normality they hoped eventually to attain.

For Anne "cross-dressing" was something she had done subconsciously all her life, feeling as she did, comfortable only when she was wearing the inevitable pair of trousers. She had ventured into menswear shops and her clothes were cut for men or at best unisex. It was easy enough to dress as a man without making much by way of radical change, except for cutting short her shoulder length hair.

As spring turned to summer so they emerged like young butterflies hesitant yet full of excited anticipation as to how they would be received. At first, it was easier to venture out at night into the city, into the dimly lit anonymity of the clubs and discotheques, merging with their cosmopolitan pool of customers. It was a glossy, fantastic environment, one to which most people flocked for enjoyable escapism from everyday life. While those around them were for the most part preoccupied with social niceties, busy in idle pretence of one sort or another, Anne and Eugene revelled in the chance to be nothing more than their true selves.

Self-conscious of their dress, convinced that they were particularly conspicuous, they stuck closely together, not daring to mix with anyone for fear of being discovered.

Apart from appearance, there were other obvious discrepancies which could not be so easily disguised, the most revealing being their voices. On these occasions Eugene's naturally lively chatter was silenced and he barely uttered a word. Anne, ostensibly the male, had to contend with buying tickets, ordering drinks. Her voice tone was pleasant but undoubtedly feminine, and during those first few months the answer seemed to be to say and do as little as possible. If that meant going thirsty, so much the better, since it spared them the still greater horror of having to venture to the toilet.

For the moment then, this was to be a time of testing the temperature of the water; nowhere was that easier than in the convivial atmosphere of the Gay Centre discotheque, where a mixture of customers, of varying sexual persuasions and preference, gathered in comparative freedom. In such surroundings no one cared to ask questions, or even appeared to notice that Anne and Eugene might not be all they physically appeared; in fact, they seemed to accept them very much as the couple had hoped, clothed as they were in the dress of their true identities.

The centre was nothing if not understanding of the needs of its clientele, there was even a changing room and toilets set aside for the use of transvestites, so that no one should be unduly embarrassed.

Both of them felt a real exhilaration in being able to appear in public as their true selves at last. If they could not entirely relax, it nevertheless proved that their theories were undoubtedly correct and that with their indentities swopped in this way, they were far more comfortable with themselves than they had ever been in their lives before.

For Anne there was now an additional strain, for once they had moved house and Emma was settled, she returned to part-time social work. She now found herself maintaining her professional stance in the role by which people generally knew her, as a woman, and therefore, like Eugene, she began to live a truly double life; a woman at work by day, a man by night.

'It was a tremendous strain but enormously exciting, for it was my first real taste of being the right way round. Sometimes people thought we were two men, but we didn't really care, we knew that what we were doing was absolutely right.'

Even so, it was an imposing discipline by any standards and while at that stage Anne may have been mentally capable of coping, physically the strain of pregnancy and the caesarian had left her weak.

As the year progressed, as baby Emma grew and the pattern of their changing roleplay continued, so she endeavoured to find a full-time post. Money was extremely tight, their house was proving difficult to sell and stood empty for some twelve months. Furthermore, the martial arts school was floundering badly, for Tim Ward appeared to have lost interest in favour of other more lucrative business ventures within the same field; at the end of the summer he went on holiday to the Canary Isles, leaving Eugene and Michael in overall charge of both the classes and the funds.

It was to prove a disastrous move, for while the brothers were more than capable of coping with the tuition, they were hopeless with money, and by now reputedly so. Collecting the cash was a detail they largely overlooked; and as Tim usually paid for the use of the premises regularly, either on the night or by monthly invoice, he returned to find the school in disarray, with a stream of irate caretakers demanding to be paid.

The school struggled on for a while, but it was the end of the road as far as Tim was concerned. He had lost his enthusiasm and, if they were to succeed, the clubs needed constant close supervision, which he no longer had the time to give them. He therefore offered the school to the Lungs for a nominal sum; but they had no capital and maintained that in any case, they were owed money. Whatever the intracacies of the situation the school finally folded, leaving the brothers jobless. Michael was eventually to reopen the classes at Bournville, building up a school which has continued to this day.

For Eugene it was something of a mixed blessing, for Kung Fu was no longer his whole life. There were other pressing considerations not least of which was Emma, and his gradual

135

metamorphosis into womanhood. The compromise seemed to be to continue with his martial arts privately, taking individual pupils whom he could charge for the privilege of exclusive tuition. It was to prove a satisfactory solution, for the rambling back garden at the Handsworth house was an ideally secluded spot for both practice and lessons and a number of Eugene's keen and more able students were to take up the option of staying with their Master. Liz was one who fell by the wayside and with whom the couple lost touch, for it was too far for her to travel to the class at Bournville, nor was she interested in taking private lessons. Anne no longer used the bank where Liz worked as a clerk and Liz had no idea of their new address, so the friendship dwindled and was eventually lost. 'It was a great pity, we'd always got on well, Anne and I. But it was just one of those things. We both had our own busy lives, although I often thought about her and wondered what had happened to them all.'

There was, during this eventful year, one further reminder of the past for Andrew finally convinced that his wife would never return to him and that his marriage was completely over, came to visit, this time in search of a divorce.

It was infuriating, not to say ironic, to be asked to sign papers acknowledging Anne's adultery and citing Eugene as the guilty third party. For given their sexual propensities neither had ever regarded their affair as being in any way adulterous; Eugene was by no means the "other man" – if anything, the other woman. In the event, and some months later, Anne was to find herself well and truly divorced, a fact that only came to light and much to her surprise during the legalities of selling the house at Stetchford. On grounds of desertion, Andrew could divorce Anne without her consent after two years' separation. It was of no real consequence to her; she was relieved to be free and on acceptable terms.

15

As their daughter began to take notice of the world around her, to sit and crawl and identify with people and with objects, so she grew to recognize her parents; only to her, Eugene was Mother or Mummy and Anne her Father, her Daddy. From the first, that is how she was to know them and react accordingly. To Emma it was to become the natural order of things and to her parents, the most realistic way they could be effective as their true selves. However, it was with some considerable anxiety that they realized their transformations now needed to be progressed with all possible haste. As things stood there was a danger Emma would grow up amid confusion, uncertain as to the exact nature of the two people she loved and relied upon most. It was vital that they did their utmost to prevent such a dreadful situation arising; it required positive and drastic action.

Their experiences at night had only confirmed the value of what they felt within, and with their self confidence boosted in this way, they decided to find out whether medical science was prepared to offer more definite help.

The knowledge they had so far acquired about the physical process of transsexualism was fairly piecemeal, gathered from a minimal amount of contact with one or two self-help groups and from a variety of books which touched on the subject without being particularly informative. As they were soon to discover, transsexualism was a subject of which few people could claim to have experience and the medical world remained, for the most part, in ignorance.

They were to meet one transsexual who gave them fair warning of what to expect; formerly a male but now, thanks to sex change operations, totally female, she lived within the city and willingly agreed to give her advice. Eugene cross-dressed for the occasion, for he needed some independent reassurance that he had the physical potential to become an attractive and plausible female.

The woman was agreeably convinced by his appearance which, despite the voice, conveyed to her the essential prerequisites of femininity.

Not that her encouragement was without a goodly measure of caution; she told them candidly that it would be difficult, more difficult than they might ever imagine; but if they were determined to go ahead, then she would tell them how to go about finding doctors who were willing to help.

They came away feeling on the one hand newly elated, yet on the other apprehensive; it was to be some time before they acted on her advice.

1978 arrived and with it Emma's first birthday. They both knew that they had to forge ahead. It was a strangely harrowing position to be in; for as much as they longed to become full and complete in their true sexual roles, they were so alarmed at the thought of rejection by the doctors, that they hardly dared to make that initial approach.

For what if medical opinion was against them? What if the very people who held the key to their future refused to give them the vital treatment? The result would be unimaginable; to be left in physical limbo, to be trapped always within the wrong framework, making futile attempts to convince everyone, Emma included, of their proper gender.

It was therefore with great trepidation that they made an appointment with a psycho-sexual counsellor. The Brook Centre, where the counsellor worked voluntarily, was a mere stone's throw from home, yet it took great courage to make the short journey.

As it turned out, there was nothing to fear. In their brief chat with the counsellor the woman could offer no more than information, for transsexualism was a subject she confessed to knowing little about. Still, they had not been rebuffed and, more positively, the counsellor had recommended them to a consultant psychiatrist who might be able to give them practical help. However cursory and inconclusive the interview, they had not, as Anne and Eugene had feared, been rejected out of hand.

138

It was to be some months before letters were exchanged and the couple were referred for appointment to the consultant's counselling clinic. When they did eventually meet, Dr S proved to be approachable but busy, he could offer them only ten minutes' consultation that day – and in viewing them for the first time was himself thrown into confusion by the complexity of a dual transsexual relationship.

'He asked us which of us was which? And who wanted to become what? It was all rather comical, but at the time we were too uptight for that to register.'

There was no time for the gruelling and in depth psychoanalysis for which they had been steeling themselves; yet judging by their appearances and on the little he knew, the consultant recommended them to an endocrinologist, whose specialist knowledge of the body's glandular system would enable him to judge their hormonal needs and prescribe accordingly.

It was an encouraging step forward to be accepted at face value by a medical consultant who apparently found them worthy of being taken seriously. A further link in the chain had also been promised and even if there was the inevitable delay, there was surely room for optimism.

In the meantime, Eugene, ever impatient and worried, too, over Emma, determined to do something to improve his appearance. For a while he took meticulous care with his grooming. His colouring was naturally dark and his beard growth profuse. First thing in the morning he was unmistakably male and although as yet Emma was hardly able to differentiate, her parents were afraid that she might form impressions that could have serious repercussions later in her life. Besides, Eugene was eager now to progress by whatever means were available, and one instant answer was electrolysis.

The treatment was intricate, painful and expensive, all good reasons for it to be avoided; but by now both Eugene and Anne were in need of a morale booster and so Eugene, with Anne along for support, began a series of sessions.

It was an embarrassing procedure, presenting himself for a treatment usually requested by women, yet at this stage not wishing to reveal his true purpose. It was also painful in the extreme and left his face tender for some days; still, the clinic's staff were used to being discreet and no hint of curiosity was shown as to why Eugene should want his beard removed, all of which helped to make his agony more bearable.

The results however, were disappointing. The successful removal of hair follicles, particularly those encouraged to grow by continuous shaving, relies on first growing the hair to a workable length and thereafter on continuous and often prolonged treatment. At six pounds per session, their limited resources could not run beyond the month and so Eugene was forced to quit. What little had been achieved was a noticeable improvement, but it was hardly sufficient to make any real difference. Realizing Eugene's despair, the clinic offered ideas on suitable cosmetics to help cover his stubble. The couple's disappointment and frustration at being hampered by lack of money was checked only by the eventual promise of their next appointment with the consultant.

Life was not spent in idle contemplation of what might or might not be in store. Anne was kept busy at work and her growing experience made her eligible for promotion to a senior grade. However unless she returned to a full-time post, this was clearly out of the question, and so finding such a job became a priority. Status apart, she desperately needed the money, for Eugene's income was, to say the least, sporadic and there was now a lively toddler to support, not to mention the Browns, who continued to hover dangerously near to the breadline. The chance to return to working full-time soon arose, but the promotion she had hoped for proved elusive. Anne and Eugene tried not to dwell too long on this for they knew that on balance what mattered most was to pursue their plans as best they could; to prepare themselves for the greater impact hormone treatment would hopefully provide.

A colleague at work, in whom Anne had confided, produced an article concerning a transsexual clinic which was being run at one of London's largest teaching hospitals. It gave the couple fresh encouragement, for here were medics who obviously were sympathetic and who, in certain cases, offered sex change surgery paid for by the National Health Service. Embracing the old cliché of "nothing ventured, nothing gained", Anne wrote in her professional capacity to the hospital's senior social worker from whom she felt certain she could expect a reply.

Explaining her and Eugene's predicament, she asked for advice; within a few days she and Eugene found themselves on the train for London, not to see any medical expert, but the social worker to whom Anne had written. Neither of them had any idea whether the trip would come to anything, but out of politeness and curiosity they felt it important to make the visit. Any new information they might glean about what was surgically possible and also about what forms of treatment were freely available would undoubtedly represent some progress.

As with Dr S, there was some initial confusion, for the social worker had never met a transsexual couple before, only helpless individuals who sought the final gratification of the sex change operation.

She proved to be a fund of information about the anatomical possibilities, the length and complexities of treatment, all of which the couple absorbed eagerly. As they listened to the cold, clinical details of converting penis to vagina, clitoris to penis, of removing breasts and building muscle, they felt not so much alarmed by the radical nature of the exercise, as exhilarated to know that so much was possible, and available.

One thing became apparent: despite Anne and Eugene's intuitions, no one, not even the medical experts, completely understood how or why transsexualism occurred. It remained something of a mystery to medical science and the social worker asked the couple whether they could explain what had caused them both to feel as they did. Just as it was something of a revelation to discover that no one seemed to have definitive answers, so Anne and Eugene found it difficult to express what it was that made them so certain they needed help. All they knew was that they both felt undeniably wrong, that in no respect did their bodies match the "inside image" that they had of themselves.

The social worker told the couple that, to be accepted as patients by the hospital, they would have initially to come recommended by their own doctor. Armed with this information they returned to Birmingham, flushed with the excitement of such a promising meeting, intrigued by the notion that despite enormous advancements in other fields of psychological and sexual disorders, medical science was only beginning to come to terms with the problems, causes and effects of transsexualism.

While Anne and Eugene waited to see the endocrinologist, there seemed to be no harm in approaching their own doctor for the necessary referral. She was understanding, and although clearly taken aback by their request – transsexualism is not one of the more common problems to confront a general practitioner – to her credit she nonetheless took them seriously.

'We were the first transsexuals she'd ever come across and we expected her to be reluctant to help us; so we were very surprised when she agreed to write to the hospital, recommending that at least they have a look at us.'

At last the wheels were being set in motion and they found themselves finally booked in for assessment with the endocrinologist, Dr K. It seemed that all the years of frustration were drawing to an end.

For Eugene in particular, the time was long overdue; despite the cross-dressing, the studied appearance with long hair, beard concealed now by careful make-up, on the frequent outings where he faced public scrutiny, he felt awkward and ungainly, his taut frame muscle-bound through endless physical training, his voice low and unreservedly manly.

For him feminine clothing provided only a limited disguise in comparison with what Anne could achieve, and more radical steps needed to be taken if he was to remain sane. As the couple's plan had evolved and the promise of treatment had become more likely, so he had grown more impatient with himself, more aware than ever of his shortcomings as a full woman and more anxious to present to his daughter a credible image as her mother. Eugene in particular then, was living on his nerves, obsessed with becoming more feminine, terrified that somewhere along the way his hopes would be dashed.

For once, things seemed to be going Anne and Eugene's way. Dr K also proved to be unexpectedly cooperative; although his main preoccupation was in dealing with diabetic illnesses, he had, from time to time discreetly helped others in a similar dilemma to theirs and in principle was willing to prescribe treatment. His encouragement was tinged with warning, however: hormone treatment rarely had a dramatic effect and the couple must on no account expect any great changes in their bodies. They would not be transformed overnight and, indeed, there was a serious risk that a course of hormone treatment would have very disappointing results.

Having thus, as he thought, tempered their expectations, the doctor gave them both a thorough examination, questioning them about their past medical history. Did either of them suffer from nervous disorders or epileptic fits? On examining Eugene he remarked on the growth pattern of his pubic hair, for it differed between the sexes and in his case was markedly feminine. This was, felt Eugene, some visible confirmation of his true identity. Dr K prescribed a course of treatment: the drugs would be available at regular intervals by prescription and via their own doctor. Barely heeding or caring unduly about his timely caution, Anne and Eugene felt jubilant, in their own words, 'literally over the moon.'

It seemed incredible that they were actually and positively embarking on the first physical step towards their goal, that contrary to expectations, and notwithstanding the long periods of waiting between consultations, convincing the medical profession of the seriousness and urgency of their intentions had not been as difficult as they had imagined. Perhaps the general impression they made had been more positive for Anne's professional standing and the fact that she held a responsible job. In any case, they were so impervious to criticism, so intent in their joint determination to fulfill their hopes together, and so apparently rational in their arguments, that no one could have been left in any doubt that they meant to succeed.

In all the consultations they endured and were to endure, Anne and Eugene were able to present a sober and sincere conviction. They fully appreciated the implications of what they were seeking to do, but considered their quest absolutely necessary. No one they had to satisfy that they were responsible people in need of medical treatment could remain sceptical for long.

Their outward image as a couple could only have helped. In a superficial way they were already beginning to look their true parts, Anne taller and somewhat heavier than Eugene, who was of a slender and not unattractive frame, with a good facial bone structure. It was hardly difficult to imagine them conforming to what they considered their true identities; indeed the initial confusion doctors tended to feel when meeting Anne and Eugene for the first time argued their case very effectively. It also provided the occasional moment of comic relief in a situation in which the couple rarely found anything to laugh at.

16

Having started treatment, and cleared what they assumed would be their greatest hurdle, Anne and Eugene now found much to consider carefully. The transition from male to female and vice versa was a major, little understood psychological phenomenon which could go horribly wrong if it was rushed. It would need to be a steady and planned progression, one which would allow them to live in comparative harmony while the hormones gradually took effect. Eugene remained optimistic that crossing over would be easy and drew great confidence from the drugs, the female hormones that he felt certain would alter his physique more drastically than the doctor had supposed. Anne remained cautious and held a less rosy view of the coming months. Imperceptibly yet swiftly she was becoming caught up in the traditionally masculine role of family provider, but in tandem with this inevitable shift in their respective roles came the nagging fear that their plans might well jeopardize her job.

It was something Anne could ill afford, for they still had large debts to clear and there was Emma to consider; she would need some financial security and in the coming years the love and constant attention that might prove difficult to sustain with any tolerance once they both began treatment in earnest. Anne and Eugene had little idea of the kind of side effects they might suffer, how they would react emotionally as the chemistry began to work. They were stepping into unknown territory, very much among the pioneers; there was very little documented experience for patients or physicians to draw upon.

It seemed probable that Eugene would take longer to adjust to the hormones, that his masculinity would take longer to disappear as the oestrogen worked its way gradually into his system, transforming his body into the female form he desired so much. Anne was already able to pass herself off, superficially at least, as a male and therefore if they began the process together, it would have to be finely balanced if they were to avoid both looking simultaneously masculine. Apart from other considerations, it would obviously be harmful for Emma to have two male-looking parents at any given time.

After some deliberation it was decided that while Eugene went straight ahead with his changeover, Anne would postpone her treatment for a while longer, at least until Eugene became more womanly. In the meantime she could support Eugene and concentrate all her energies on helping him to cope with the initial changes in his body without the additional concern of what was happening to herself; it would allow them a breathing space.

Given one injection of the male hormone, testosterone, Anne was amazed at the psychological impact it made on her. 'I felt so good, surging with strength and full of energy, as though I could've bounced high off the ground, it was absolutely marvellous.'

Reluctantly, for this first true taste of manhood had made more of an impact than she had forseen, Anne wrote to Dr K. and to the London hospital informing them of her decision to wait a while. Once she was satisfied that treatment was available, Anne was prepared for a delay.

Some of the means by which man could become woman, woman become man were now at their disposal; but there was more to the process than popping pills or being given injections. More than their bodies would have to change, if the transformation was going to be a success; patterns of behaviour differ markedly between the sexes and it was essential for Anne and Eugene to identify masculine and feminine traits and to retrain their instincts.

In their excursions to the city nightspots they had so far reacted as they saw fit without much thought to what can be described as conventional behaviour, in any case had always been very discreet and reserved to avoid embarrassment. Now, if they were to be credible, they had to examine themselves and their attitudes in the minutest detail and work to make some of the hardest adjustments of all instinctive.

Many of our actions are habitual, learnt originally from

146

observing and copying our elders, subsequently developed and refined before being assimilated into our individual make-up.

For Anne and Eugene, this had been an unnatural process, corrupting what they knew to be true of themselves. Anne had been required to identify with feminine instincts, Eugene with male, but always against their instincts. The associations were never reflexive but instead demanded continual, conscious effort. It meant that they were always acting a part.

Now they had to single out the responses that were natural to them from those which had just been part of the charade. They had also to decipher what in their behaviour was female, what male, and what if at all neutral.

Such close self-examination was nothing new to Anne, for through her work she was involved in helping many of her clients to analyse their problems and to adjust accordingly.

It would be a slow, tedious process and one demanding constant reappraisal; to begin with they decided it was best to concentrate on one or two of the major differences most easily pinpointed between the sexes, namely walking and talking. Making surreptitious mental notes of anyone and everyone they came across in their daily round, they began comparing themselves critically to others, and wherever necessary, making a change.

Talking was infinitely complex, for speech patterns differ considerably between men and women, and while Eugene was naturally loquacious and already had something resembling a female giggle, he needed to separate his phrasing less deliberately, without annunciating too fast; whereas Anne needed to check the pace of her speech. It was no use them copying one another, for that would only lead to total chaos; but at least, if only through habit, each could advise the other on ways of improvement.

The problem of voice pitch was something that only speech therapy and the hormones could improve and even now it needlessly remains one of Eugene's greatest worries.

Walking presented less of a problem, for with continuous practice it easily improved. Anne's observations of men made her realize that the majority of them took fairly long and purposeful strides whereas hers were comparatively short; from then on it became a policy to make herself take longer strides whenever she went out.

'I was surprised to find that right from the outset walking in this new way felt more relaxing and natural. For a month or two I made a conscious effort to think about what I was doing, but then one day I realized that it was no longer something I had to specifically think about; I was automatically taking bigger steps and I felt quite at ease doing so.

'It made me recognize that until then I had always felt a certain amount of tension and uneasiness when out walking – especially when I was with someone – now I found that I felt much more relaxed.'

As one mannerism improved, so they found the project snowballed, for as they made progress in one area so it became necessary to alter in others. Eating and table habits were harder to adapt, for in general men naturally eat faster and more singlemindedly than women, who usually make some concession to daintiness, reluctant on the whole to demonstrate too healthy an appetite.

At first Eugene went over the top in his attempt to eat graciously, little finger upturned at every excuse, pushing his food around in finicky fashion without actually eating much. Based on the impression that men generally gulped and shovelled their food down with some alacrity, Anne speeded up her eating, considerably.

Less apparent to the outside world but no less important to the overall picture were the more intimate changes. For Eugene it became so vital to be feminine in every sense of the word, that he quickly took to sitting rather than standing when he urinated, even when desperate. The basic act of using the lavatory is often a crisis for male transsexuals, who were constantly reminded of their gender by the process of urination; by adopting the female position so resolutely, Eugene found it easier to establish himself as a woman, and avoided jarring reminders of his physical masculinity at frequent intervals throughout the day.

Out of this jungle of human patterning, Anne and Eugene hoped to find themselves presenting to society two acceptable beings who would not be marked as freaks or failures by the slightest deviation from normal behaviour. From the moment they began hormonal treatment the couple lived with the belief – almost an obsession – that society had them under close scrutiny from that point onwards and the smallest mistake could leave them open to hostility and suspicion.

'We had to calculate our deficiencies in one area – for both of us the most difficult was the voice – and compensate for it in another, so that overall the effect was right. People are on the whole very bright and we had to be credible.'

While it may seem inconsistent for two people to be determindly unconventional in tackling their gender problems so radically, yet anxious to conform in other respects, this was by no means illogical.

For in the process of "unlearning" the attitudes that had cluttered the façade of their lives to date, they were revelling in the delight of discovery; as Anne and Eugene gradually adopted the social stance of their true genders, so their belief grew that they were no longer play-acting, for every new mannerism felt absolutely natural and not in the slightest way contrived. Their burgeoning confidence only served to enhance the feelings of completeness for which they were constantly striving and which was vital if they were ever to enjoy full and happy lives. At the same time it was of paramount concern to both her parents that Emma should grow up in a normal and stable environment, and for Anne and Eugene to be accepted and assimilated by society seemed the surest means by which this could be achieved. Ironically in many ways, it was Emma who helped her parents achieve credibility, for the presence of a small child, and a personable little soul at that, did much to enable the family to conform to the conventional image of normality.

Indeed, that was how family life had become and how they had always wished and expected that it would be. While Eugene found it harder than he had imagined to cope with the pressures of crossing over, he had longed for this child and had no intention of abdicating his responsibilities as her mother. He was solicitous in his care of Emma, continuing as he had began, to cater for all her daily needs. Anne remained totally supportive, if more distanced, and between them they bestowed on Emma all the love and affection she could have wished for, a love she quickly reciprocated.

In every way then, a promising family life was beginning to fashion on a more solid foundation for itself. Eugene and Anne saw the possibility of escaping the trap of their false bodies open up before them; the future was starting to fall into place.

As Eugene began to take his daily dosage of hormone he became fancifully obsessed with any signs of change.

'It was crazy, I kept looking in the mirror expecting to see someone different staring back at me. I had such faith in what I was doing and in those pills, I was totally impatient for some results.'

It was to be some months before the first signs were noticeable; a sharp pain in his chest heralded the sprouting of breasts, which at first were no more than "little molehills". Simultaneously his skin texture began to soften, his facial features slowly to alter and lose their angularity.

For the moment his expectations of what crossing over would entail, the depth of insight and the degree of psychological adjustment that had to be achieved, fell far short of reality. After more than twenty-five years of pretence, it was a wonderful but also awesome experience to allow himself complete freedom of expression, to exercise all that had gone on before.

Anne and Eugene decided that to complement their first steps on the path to new physical forms they ought to take new names, which would symbolize a complete break with the past. They drew up lists of suitable suggestions, rejecting many out of hand as too obvious, others plain ridiculous. A current hit in the pop charts was the musical version of Emily Brontë's classic, "Wuthering Heights", performed by the highly individual singer, Kate Bush.

The song told of the disastrous love affair between Heathcliffe and Cathy; it was played incessantly on radio and television. Kate and Cathy or Catherine were all names Eugene found appealing and after some prevarication he settled for Catherine, or Cathy for short – and so Eugene Brown, alias Eugene Sifu C. Lung now became Catherine Brown.

For Anne and Eugene life had become an exhilarating experience in a way it had never been before; and they now found a way of expressing themselves that was as spirited as it was exciting.

Eugene's changeover coincided with the emergence of the Punk Movement amongst Britain's young. Theirs was a world aggressively anti-establishment, depicted most vividly through brash music and outrageous dress, and one which at that time was formed more or less at random, with little expectation that it would develop to gain the widespread acceptance and acclaim which it now enjoys.

Primarily its appeal for Anne and Cathy lay in the opportunity it offered them for disguise, if that was what they needed, during the interim period that their bodies were altering. The heavy and often bizarre make-up used by the girls would help Cathy overcome the problem of her complexion which still threatened Cathy's attempts to *be* a young woman in the eyes of others.

Beardline carefully concealed with make-up, eyes suitably coloured and adorned with shadows and mascara, her dress studiously chosen to be outlandishly punk, she and Anne, dressed more sombrely, yet still in keeping, ventured to their first punk concert.

It had already taken some contrivance to achieve the desired effect; buying cosmetics was in itself an ordeal, and although Anne despised make-up and had given up wearing it for herself long ago, of necessity she sometimes went out to buy for Cathy. Neither of them had much idea of what they were looking for, other than that it needed to be particularly heavy in texture and capable of dealing with problems that manufacturers scarcely considered. It was difficult to discuss Cathy's requirements with salesgirls going into detail, but eventually after some trial and error, they managed to find something to suit.

Over the next few months they were to make frequent trips together to the department store where they made their purchases, always arousing curiosity as to who exactly they were buying for and yet eventually becoming accepted by the assistants for what they were. Duly prepared for their first visit to a rock concert, they mingled easily among the young audience. They had already explored the fringes of the punk world and had found they liked the music. Now the concert proved to be something of a turning point, for the raw excitement of the group "X-Ray Specs" and the brilliant vocals of their lead singer, the amazing Polystyrene, invoked an atmosphere charged with electricity.

Clad in her "X-Ray Specs" t-shirt, Cathy was euphoric to hear someone draw attention to her in the crowd.

'I heard them say, "Look, she's wearing one of their shirts, doesn't she look good?" They'd called me "she", that's what I was thrilled about, it was the first time anyone had referred to me automatically as a female.'

Anne and Eugene, now Cathy, came away from that concert elated. Ten years of frustration had begun to slip from their shoulders. It had been a milestone occasion.

It was this fresh charge that led them to further self-analysis. Talking over the concert on the way home it occurred to Anne and Cathy that as teenagers neither of them had ever felt free to let themselves go with the normal irresponsibility of youth. There had been little room in their early lives for self-exploration, partly because uninhibited self-expression would have forced them to reveal all the doubts they had felt about their roles in life at a time when they were hardly mature enough to cope. At the same time neither Anne nor Eugene had wanted to develop much within the limitations of their apparent sex and they had therefore found themselves excluded from the youth they would dearly have loved to have been a part of – Anne as a wilful adolescent boy, Eugene as a girl in the first intriguing stages of womanhood.

Perhaps now there was a chance to catch up on that missed experience. Neither of them looked their age, and while it would be impossible to recreate everything as if they were back in their teens, it seemed feasible to imagine that the punks could offer them the chance to be young awhile. It would, they felt, be valuable therapy, for in attempting to adjust to a new adulthood, they would need to draw on the values and knowledge normally gained in the process of growing up. Despite their instinctive awareness of how they personally felt, Anne and Cathy thought it was only commonsense that no man could reach proper maturity without first being a boy, nor a woman without making her discoveries and mistakes as a girl.

They mused on how life might have been if they had been allowed to grow up naturally. Both had always been interested in pop music, in fashion; Anne felt sure that she would have been a strident "Mod". She had secretly longed to be one of those clean-cut lads who had patrolled on scooters, dressed and ready for action in the event of coming face to face with their arch enemies, "the Rockers". Though some of the current punk fashions were perhaps too extreme, the clothes were nonetheless cheap and easily available, the music was exhilarating, and above all, the punks themselves were far more liberated in their views than the couple's contemporaries. If any punk should ever suspect that Anne and Cathy were not all they seemed, it was unlikely that the discovery would be considered worth getting excited about!

Anne and Cathy found it convenient to adopt the punk style of dress, particularly while their bodies remained in such an androgynous state. The quicker they could begin to be accepted for what they really were, the more their confidence would grow and the faster their psychological transformation would progress.

At first, punk or not, their expeditions into the outside world were brief and tentative, though each time they ventured out was another hurdle overcome. To be recognized as a member of their true sex was in every respect mind-blowing, and even the simple act of being addressed as "Sir" instead of "Madam", as "son" rather than "love", gave Anne a shock of pleasure, not just at the time but for days afterwards as she recalled the incident.

The couple remained severely hampered by their ill-matched voices, caught in a state of terror whenever the necessity arose to hold a conversation of any length. On one occasion, the bewilderment of a young salesman in a record store left Cathy particularly upset. 'It was our voices that confused him, and I suppose it was funny and at the same time embarrassing. Anyway, from then on I decided to shut my mouth and put a tin lid on it. After that whenever we went out I'd just cling on, almost as if I was recoiling; people must've thought I was dumb or anti-social – that I must've had something wrong in the head.'

The same thing happened again when Cathy was standing in a bus queue. Two youths were obviously determined to bait her: 'They yelled out from the back of the queue, "Ah, that girl's a guy", and so I was shown up to the rest of the passengers. I hated having to go on that bus, it was a terrible strain at the time, I felt as if the eyes of the world were upon me.'

17

For Anne, still patiently awaiting her chance to start treatment, the delay was inordinately difficult. Changing her name would give her a fillip and a new status which she badly needed to establish now, not only socially but also at work. She had already admitted to a select few of her colleagues that she intended to become a man and had been met by a general reaction of blank amazement. Indeed, when the chance of promotion eventually arose, her interview was inexplicably postponed.

'When I asked why, they said what else did I expect. Because of what I was, some of the men were worried about which toilets I'd use. It dawned on me that from then on I was bound to meet resistance.'

She had expected more sympathy from people whose prime function was to help socially inadequate and the deprived. Still, it became apparent that some of her male colleagues regarded her as a threat, although some of the more concerned among them confessed, with misplaced gallantry, that they liked her well enough the way she was, queried why she could want to do such a thing, and warned Anne that she would never succeed.

'Like social workers everywhere they were always reluctant to discuss their own problems, as if they were too busy coping with everyone else's, and that to admit to having any of your own was in many ways an admission of failure.'

The apparent disinterest and scepticism of her colleagues only drove Anne to prove them wrong and the way to find out if she could ever be accepted professionally as a man, Anne decided, was to leave 'Anne' behind forever and to take a new name. She chose the inoffensive and slightly ambiguous name of Christopher, which shortened to Chris could be taken for either sex. Now she was determined to see whether her chances of being accepted as a male improved; she even had business cards printed on which she firmly pronounced herself to be Chris Johnson.

This demonstrative step coincided with the chance of a senior post in an area of the neighbouring town of Wolverhampton. She was to become an out-of-hours duty officer, which meant being on call during unsocial hours, during the night and the usual holiday periods. It was inconvenient and involved travelling some distance, but if it enabled her to move up to a full-time senior's job then Chris was prepared to put up with the inconvenience.

At first, the assumption at the district office where she was based was that Chris Johnson was a liberated female, though gradually more and more of her clients took her to be a man. In any event, the emergence of Cathy and Chris was a symbolic end to their previous existence; they had always regarded one another as "she" and "he" in accordance with the identities they had adopted with Emma. Therefore in writing of their life together, it is timely to change our reference; henceforth Anne will be referred to as Chris, the man, and Eugene as Cathy, the woman and mother of Emma.

Chris was thankfully embarking on a particularly busy period, for towards the end of 1978 he managed to secure for himself a full-time and permanent position; this time, thanks to the amount of overtime he had put in, they could hardly refuse him. He did not give up all of the out of hours work, for it represented some valuable overtime and while it was tiring, it was not unduly demanding, most of the night being spent on administrative paperwork.

Social work was something he found infinitely enjoyable and which by all accounts, he was good at; for he showed his clients compassion and understanding, a special sympathy grown out of his own dilemma.

Work was a major preoccupation, fulfilling and in the meantime there was Emma to consider, not to mention the need to mix and enjoy themselves socially in the heady and carefree atmosphere of punk society.

In many ways it was as if their lives had indeed begun again and suddenly held enormous fresh promise. The bonds of their joint affection were, if anything, growing stronger, cemented by young Emma who remained a delightful if exhausting commitment. It was their continuing, growing love affair that inspired Chris and Cathy to start writing songs, romantic, sentimental notions which seem to mirror their changing fortunes and circumstances.

The words were simple, yet often indicative of their singular predicament, as in this from "The First Time" (That I Met You)':

Two strangers came together
Each with their own disguise,
They can't ignore the truth somehow
When they're touching with their eyes.
I fear you'll slip away from me
Like pebbles through the sand,
These moments may be all we have
And I need to touch your hand.
I think that I'm in love.

Later, the frustrations of being trapped within the wrong body were to be epitomized in "Ms Robot", a pitiful little ditty that offers a glimpse of their continuing and underlying despair:

They call me Ms Robot
I was project Number One,
A walking, talking robot
But I want to have some fun.
Somebody screwed me together,
Put microcircuits in my head.
I can count with the speed of lightning
But nobody ever shares my bed.
I see people laughing,
I see lovers holding hands.
But I was created by this mad scientist
And I have to do whatever she commands.
All day long I work things out for her,
Hundreds of sums that she can't do.
She asks me what to eat for breakfast
And what to wear in the evening too.
One day I'm gonna be happy.
Some day I'm gonna be free.
Won't somebody switch my circuits
Then I can find the real me.

157

By now the treatment was beginning to have more tangible effects on Cathy, so that even some of her Kung Fu pupils began to notice a difference in her. The pills she took every day now as a matter of course, were supplemented when she eventually managed to obtain an appointment with the London hospital and with the consultant psychiatrist who was reputed to be one of the few authorities on transsexualism in the country.

It was a strange encounter, for even the ordeal of travelling to London and presenting herself for professional scrutiny was exhausting. So much depended upon the initial impression and upon her ability to exude a self-confidence in her chosen role.

The appointment was not unlike a severe cross-examination, ruthless in its candour and almost scathing in its attack. There were no physical examinations or clinical tests, but at least Cathy came away with the promise of further help and the vague impression that an operation might eventually be forth-coming, provided she adhered strictly to the consultant's requirements.

Cathy was given no chance to enquire further into the implications of the consultant's broad proviso, for the clinic was a full one and the consultant busy with the other sad and ambiguous looking characters who waited their turn uncertainly outside.

New drugs had been prescribed which were stronger and more potent, and the effects on Cathy were more dramatic than she had expected, particularly on her general physical condition. The superb physical strength and agility she had acquired through the martial arts began to ebb. Try as she did to maintain her fitness and mobility, she found herself growing weaker, incapable of performing the feats she had always tackled so easily.

'I was frightened. It'd never occurred to me that women simply don't have the same potential body strength or stamina as men, and I felt helpless as all my power just drained away. I still expected my body to work as it had done before, but that became more and more hopeless.'

The tensions that this created were almost unbearable, for as she pushed herself to match her past achievements, so her chest was pierced with a pain so excruciating that Cathy felt herself growing faint. It was as if her muscular frame was being contorted and contracted from within into more rounded female contours. Even her skintone was losing its darkness, becoming softer and less grey. Yet there was little she could do about her rib cage which remained obstinately predominant; and with her breasts developing so nicely, it became a depressing and incessant worry. So agonized did she become that the tension hardened her body until she felt that she would burst with the pressure. It was Chris who on these occasions taught her how to breathe and relax herself, who would spend hours massaging her tight, incongruous form until she fell limp. For the pains were due to more than her physical transformation. With her failing strength, Cathy was beginning to visualize a time when she would no longer be able to continue with the martial arts. It was one side-effect she had never anticipated.

When the time came to give up martial arts, she would be giving up a pursuit that she not only loved but that had given her identity, helped established her as a person of some stature, and formed the backbone of her fragile self-confidence. It was difficult enough to endure an existence as something of an hermaphrodite, without being forced to forfeit the one thing at which she could hope to excel. For the first time since she and Chris had reached their decision, Cathy felt some measure of fear about the future.

Only within the realms of their family life with Emma did these early months of treatment seem to be carefree and reasonably uncomplicated. Chris and Cathy took their parental duty very seriously and seemed in every way like any other close-knit and loving family. With money invariably short there was little to spare for outings, but Emma loved to visit the park, to feed the ducks and play on the swings. The tedium and sheer ordinariness of their daily routine acted as a counterbalance to all else that was happening, and in concentrating their energies on bringing up their child, they were able to momentarily forget their own frustrations.

This was in itself a full time job, as the parents of every boisterous toddler know only too well. Blessed with a vivid imagination, Emma loved to play at make believe and together the three of them would be transported on flights of fantasy which they all shared. Emma's little world was very much a part of their own and since the child had no inkling of her parents' dilemma, the threesome they presented was a typical family picture to any casual observers who might have watched them playing together.

As Chris and Cathy probed their own psyches more deeply, so Chris found himself wondering about some small discrepancies in Cathy's story. There was little he could pinpoint exactly, for any inconsistency that had arisen previously had been hastily glossed over or explained away. Since her family confirmed her tale of being raised in Hong Kong, and their martial arts associates remained suitably impressed, inspired even, by her ability, there were no definable reasons for suspicion.

Her lack of concentration and somewhat undisciplined way of training had long struck Chris as irregular, given her supposedly rigorous oriental upbringing and the stern image she had presented in class. But Chris was inclined to ascribe these inconsistencies in Cathy to her preoccupation with Emma and despondency over her dwindling physical prowess.

Just how exactly he began to discover the truth about Cathy's background no one can remember. However, once he had an inkling that he had been deceived – and it was to take many months for the whole story to emerge – he felt deeply and irresolutely hurt, let down by the one person in whom he had placed an absolute, loving trust, possibly more so than usual between any couple because of the unique nature of their circumstances and dependence on each other.

The initial shock left him saddened; for it had already taken a considerable time and a great deal of patience, before Cathy would confide in him about her visionary powers, afraid as she was that he would think her mad, maybe even schizoid. Now that she had overcome her reticence and learnt not to fear sharing her foresight, they were faced with this further disclosure. Clearly Cathy was not the person he had believed her to be, nor was she quite the woman with whom he had fallen in love. Yet why had she created such an unusual and exotic past? There must surely be more deep-seated reasons for such deception than a desire to play some clever confidence trick?

Chris felt that he and Cathy had to establish total honesty between them if they were to continue with their intention to cross over. Unless Cathy was frank about her past, she would not stand a chance of coming through the sex change successfully. In the months ahead they would need to draw confidence from each other; moments of doubt, fear and physical anguish would need to be weathered together, and they could ill afford not to trust each other completely.

Until now Cathy's insecurity and lack of self-reliance had been hidden behind a smokescreen of which Eugene Sifu Lung had been a vital component, necessary if she was going to have any success at hiding her truly feminine personality and live out a sham existence as a man.

But with that pretence behind her, no longer required now that she was living openly as a woman, Cathy found herself growing increasingly unsure of her own capabilities. Though she never wavered in her convictions, the emergence of her natural female personality was being hindered by the emotional upheaval of being forced to give up that part of her past life to which she had clung, even though it was founded on a lie.

It took great courage for Cathy to reveal the full truth and during weeks of half-truths, which the Browns refused to either confirm or deny, the couple's relationship reached an 'impasse'. First trying gentle persuasion, Chris insisted that Cathy should confide in him and face reality. His efforts proved unsuccessful and he could see no way forward while the element of mistrust between them remained. Deeply unhappy at this sudden and enormous setback, Chris found himself seeking consolation elsewhere.

It began innocently enough, for when Chris turned to a woman colleague for friendship in the depth of despair, he had no intention of allowing any serious relationship to develop. Some two years older than Chris and unmarried, Elizabeth was a personable, undeniably attractive young woman who devoted all her energies to her career in social work. She thoroughly enjoyed even the more mundane tasks that her job entailed, such as taking children in council care to the dentist. A respectable, heterosexual female, she and Chris found much in common and so as his domestic situation became more distraught, so he confided to Elizabeth his troubles with Cathy.

'She knew me and respected me as a man and was incredibly understanding. It was wonderful, I'd begun to feel so alone, so alienated from Cathy.'

It was almost inevitable that they started to see one another socially; Elizabeth rented a house in Wolverhampton and although they did not go out together much – for colleagues there knew Chris as a woman and Elizabeth was anxious not to be dubbed a lesbian – they did occasionally go to the cinema. More often than not their time together was spent at the house, in animated conversation or loving affection. Neither of them had ever indulged in lesbianism, nor did they now, for Elizabeth found it impossible to regard Chris as anything other than a man. As the weeks passed, so their affair grew more serious. His and Cathy's plan seemed to be going awry, for in his wildest dreams Chris had never imagined himself in such a confused and agonizing situation, apparently deserting the woman and child he truly loved.

In his bewilderment, Chris suffered momentary doubt over his need to go through with a complete sex-change. If a devastatingly attractive and wholly woman like Elizabeth accepted him as a man as he was, perhaps there was no need to go through with all the medical treatment. But the doubt was quickly dismissed.

'That would've been a betrayal of all Cathy and I had striven for and a betrayal of myself. It was unthinkable to stop now that I had achieved so much towards my goal.'

Cursing himself for making the situation worse, yet feeling helpless to put an end to his affair, Chris was terrified. There was no doubting his affection for Elizabeth, who, in addition offered the chance of an altogether more stable existence than the topsy-turvy lifestyle that he and Cathy had to endure in the course of crossing over.

Equally there was no denying his love for Cathy to whom, as pressure of his predicament increased, Chris confessed his affair.

'I had to be completely honest with her, there was no other way. I simply couldn't keep secrets from her, especially after insisting that she be truthful to me. As for being fought over I was absolutely terrified of what was going to happen, how it'd work out.'

The complexities were aggravated by work, for Chris had a particularly heavy caseload at the time and Elizabeth's presence in the office, more than a comfort, now became a constant reminder of his infidelity. Nevertheless the liaison continued, Chris splitting his time between the two women, never pretending to Cathy, always making it clear whom he was going to see.

For Cathy, already struggling to deal with her past, trying to retain a semblance of order in Emma's routine, her body beleagured by unfamiliar pains, it was an infinitely distressing and oppressive time.

'I was literally distraught, I just didn't know what to do or how to handle it. I even made him take Emma and me to meet Elizabeth, against his better judgement, as if that would help me to understand. Admittedly she seemed a very nice person, she even said she wanted to help us, but it was all too much, I just didn't feel I had the composure to be in control.'

By now Chris himself felt demented, for he had never experienced such burdensome responsibility and the pressure became intolerable. As before in his life when the heat had become too intense, he decided to retreat, and set off, ostensibly for a weekend's camping in the isolation of the Derbyshire hills. It was to be three weeks before he returned, during which time Cathy and Elizabeth, mutually abandoned, found a common bond in their concern for his safety. They agreed that whoever heard from him first would immediately inform the other, for they both felt that, under extreme stress, Chris might be dangerously unpredictable. After ten agonizing days, a desperate Cathy left Emma in the care of her mother and, with a Rastafarian student friend, set out for Derbyshire in search of the man she loved. It proved a fruitless pilgrimage, for they didn't have the faintest notion of where to start looking amid the hundreds of square miles of peaks and dales; in the process Cathy fell and hurt her leg, was hospitalized and returned home virtually immobile.

Cathy was tempted to follow Chris' example with a gesture of defiance, and she sought to console herself over Chris' desertion in the arms of another. Bravely she allowed a young punk to make advances; it was exhilarating to find that he had no hesitation in taking her to be a woman, though Cathy did not intend to allow his advances to progress to the point where he might discover the truth.

'I s'pose I was trying to prove to Chris that two could play at his game, so I let this chap kiss me and put his arms around me – but after a week I had an attack of conscience. What was I doing? I told him to forget it, after all, I'd practically got a husband.'

The lovers were to be reunited only after an inexplicable

quirk of fate. Severely depressed, Cathy turned as ever to her God, for perhaps He could alleviate her anguish. Together with a friend she went to a Christian meeting at the Pentecostal church. The pastor's sermon told of the day of pentecost and of a great wind, a terrific storm in the hills, of tents being blown asunder, collapsing under the force of the elements.

Fearful that what she had heard spelled out danger for Chris, she cried out. Cathy was convinced it was her husband the pastor was talking about, he who had gone missing and who she wanted back so badly. By an eerie coincidence, many miles away Chris was indeed struggling to keep tent and belongings together in what was a violent, freak storm. His tent had collapsed and, realizing that any efforts to rebuild it would be futile as long as the storm kept up, he decided to break camp and return home. He had reached no decisions, but the time to himself had at least calmed his nerves.

It was Elizabeth who later drove him back to Derbyshire to collect the belongings which he had abandoned in the storm; they spent a harmonious night together under canvas, Chris fulfilled in the knowledge that he was once again being loved as a man, a delightful confirmation of his masculinity.

For a while Chris' resumed home life was reasonably peaceful, yet nothing had been resolved and when Chris broached the subject of his leaving, there was a terrific row. Cathy was at her most vulnerable when faced with the emotional crisis of what was a most extraordinary love triangle. By now she had managed to strip away all the remnants of her masculinity; almost exaggerated feminine instincts coloured her thoughts and her reactions to a situation that is a common feature of intimate human relationships.

At the very moment when the unity of purpose and strength that had been Chris and Cathy seemed about to crack, Chris suddenly understood Cathy completely for the first time, and was drawn closer to her by what he saw. What he saw was undoubtedly feminine, but by no means a woman. Instead he was confronted by the raw and complex emotions of a girl, a young girl who had never had the chance to develop emotionally into womanhood. It was as if, while her body grew older, Cathy's nature had remained frozen in time, making it impossible for her to respond to the current crisis with the maturity of an adult.

The moment heralded a breakthrough, in the couple's relationship. Neither Chris nor Cathy had previously given much thought to the emotional effects of having been trapped in the wrong bodies for all those years; it had not occurred to them that the enjoyment they found in mingling with the punk generation, years younger than themselves, held any particular significance. Now Chris began to recognize that, in discarding the false skins that were their mistaken sexes, he and Cathy had exposed two new, raw souls whose emotional ages had not kept pace with their physical ageing. Under those skins were two people who did not simply need the punk world as a means of disguise, as an uninhibited outlet for their newfound energies, or even as compensation for lost youth; rather, they had gravitated towards the punk scene in a subconscious effort to find company at the natural level of their own emotional adjustment. Except organically, Chris and Cathy were still teenagers.

As they came to terms with this concept of frozen emotions, much of the mistrust and confusion that threatened Chris and Cathy's relationship disappeared. They recognized that their transsexualism had handicapped them emotionally as well as physically, and that if they were going to keep pace with the changes to their bodies that drugs and later surgery would create, they were going to have to re-examine more than just the mannerisms and habits acquired during their early years.

In recognizing the impact of their transsexual condition on their emotional development, Chris also recognized that Cathy had probably been the harder hit. Society's more abrasive approach to its menfolk had forced her to face events and attitudes during her adolescent years that she must have been ill-equipped to endure.

There was no way now that Chris could abandon her, for she was far too defenceless; still he felt that their future together hinged on her willingness to reveal the truth about herself. Slowly, reluctantly Cathy agreed to tell Chris about her past; even then, it took twelve months of gradual, sympathetic prising to get Cathy to reveal everything.

There remained the question of Elizabeth; Chris had hardly seen her since his return, but his reluctance to finish the relationship finally persisted. Such was her compassion and her understanding, that in sharing their problems Elizabeth had come to recognize the unshakeable commitment Cathy and

Chris had made to find their true selves, and to each other, even before Chris recognized it fully himself.

She therefore suggested they meet, she and Cathy, in Handsworth Park. Knowing Chris' genuine love for this other woman, Cathy went to Handsworth prepared to concede defeat. It was with astonishment that she heard Elizabeth announce that she had decided to leave Chris.

'She said "You do still love him, don't you? Well, I love him too, but you and Emma need him more than I do, so it's for the best."' Elizabeth had made the decision for Chris.

Nevertheless, the episode had made an enormous impact on both Chris and Cathy and if his affair with Elizabeth was ever going to be put behind him Chris felt that he would have to leave his job. Since his return from his camping exile, Chris had stayed away from work, but the decision to leave the post permanently was still hard; once he resigned Chris felt it was unlikely he would find work elsewhere, given the paucity of jobs and the fact that his transsexualism could not exactly be considered an asset in any job application.

Chris had no idea how the family would manage to live without any regular income, but he knew that he and Cathy would stand no chance if he continued to live a double life.

18

The time had come for reassessment, Chris and Cathy urgently needed to examine their emotions, to try to help each other to maturity before they became locked in any kind of permanent adolescence.

The task of improving their capacity to cope with their new lives would from now on have to progress on two levels: in ordinary, practical terms and, more fundamentally, by learning to rationalize and reason through their problems in an adult way.

Yet there was nothing adult in the petulant defiance that Chris now began to demonstrate and which he directed almost singlemindedly against God. Life had become tortuously complex, and in his frustration Chris turned against what he considered to be the source of his misfortunes.

Chris and Cathy had not originally made the grave decision to proceed with sex changes without painstaking consideration of the moral implications, or without reference to God, in whom they both now firmly believe.

Indeed, religion has been an important factor in their lives.

From her earliest days Cathy, as Eugene, had embraced the Catholic faith, though at the same time despising it for its apparent hypocrisy. At the age of ten she took First Communion and at thirteen she was confirmed. Her mother had been Protestant before meeting Eugene Senior, and the family maintained their friendships in the Orange Lodge. It was in the embittered struggles between these factions that Cathy recognized something disturbing about conventional, ritualistic religion. Nevertheless instilled within her there remained an unwavering faith in the existence of the Almighty and a conviction that whatever life held in store was to a certain extent ordained by Him, and that therefore He would provide.

It was a solid religious belief that had supported her through a young life of great uncertainty and which had offered hope against all odds, particularly during those grim years spent in the training school. Praying was something she had always done, almost by instinct, something from which she drew comfort. To live without God was somehow unimaginable and even though she had never been a regular churchgoer, she had worshipped from deep within herself the Saviour she saw as her guide and mentor.

The visions and spiritual sensitivities to which she was prone and which had so startled and disrupted her as a child, served only to heighten her perception of God, of the unknown forces of good and evil and their eternal conflict within each and every human soul. Much of what she saw and later knew through these visual flashes was uncanny in its accuracy, almost as though in allowing the winsome traveller child such foresight her Maker was somehow preparing the way for all that followed. The visions of Tibet, for example, gave her credence in her chosen art of Kung Fu; the recurring reference to the woman she saw presaged her recognition of and love for Chris. Cathy regarded these "flashes" as genuine manifestations of God's intentions for her; and she felt infinitely grateful for His gift of insight.

In her long struggle to reconcile her female spirit and life force with her masculine conformity Cathy looked to God as her comforter and confidant. For was it not true that:

The Lord desires our love
In every heart He wishes to be first
He therefore keeps the secret key himself . . .
For Christ alone can satisfy the soul
And those who walk with Him from day to day
Can never have a solitary way.

For Cathy the years of inner solitude and utter dejection were only made bearable because she considered them all to be a part of God's will. She felt reassured that by maintaining her faith in Him, someday life would eventually come right. There were naturally numerous times when her faith wavered, when the frustration of feeling herself irrevocably trapped within Eugene's physical framework proved too exasperating,

168

too explosive to control. These were black times of deep depression, when despite all the diversions, she had felt unnervingly close to opting out, to taking her own life. It was a measure of her faith in God that it was always to Him that she turned at these times of abject despair. As if in His wisdom, He was testing her strength of purpose and her resolve to succeed in becoming a full woman.

She felt certain that her skills at the martial arts were by way of some compensation for the basic misdirection of her mind and body, as if the powerful attributes she attained through meditation offered her a level of self-knowledge and a transitory peace of mind that, on the whole, most people were denied.

When Buddhism was offered as an alternative, she gave it suitable scrutiny, became fascinated by its history and legend, even tried to emulate its teachings, only to eventually reject it in favour of the basic Christian ethic.

Though Cathy was continually plagued with frightening self-doubts she was able always to draw unhesitatingly on her God, to entreat His help in resolving the eternal troubles that life presented.

Conversely, Chris had no such backbone of faith to draw upon. Despite the broadly based philosophy of virtuous good living on which he had been brought up and subsequently endeavoured to live by, he had no such belief in a God or in any superior being to whom he owed an allegiance. On the contrary, if there was a God, then how did He explain Chris being born in the wrong body? If He was his maker then how could He have allowed such an aberration to occur? This was the defiant challenge which Chris as Anne threw in the face of the Almighty. Spasmodic visits to Sunday School and a passing enjoyment in singing church hymns were not enough to fully convince him of God's existence, so that by the age of sixteen a disillusionment bordering on resentment coloured his religious views.

It sprung, naturally enough, from his own dilemma, but was fanned by a growing despair at the state of the world which it seemed to him could only worsen. While Chris was in full agreement with the moral teachings of Christianity, he could find no way of equating them with the extremes of good and bad fortune that befell mankind.

This was a viewpoint shared by Andrew and for the duration

169

of their relationship they were both fervent atheists. As Anne, Chris felt that no one could show him God – the facts of life in all their harshness, the starvation and deprivation of millions, warfare and wanton violence, rendered such a deity either non-existent or, worse, cruel in the extreme.

This fairly common, radically idealistic outlook only began to be shaken by Andrew's involvement with the occult.

At the university at Keele, as his interest in the Martial Arts and Yoga developed, he became vaguely aware of the possibility of there being other realities, or forces, apart from that which was obvious or concrete: that there might well be a life force which supported and sustained the universe. Yet the idea of Christianity still made him unreasonably angry, despite the fact that as Anne, he and Andrew had known many people who professed to being Christians and occasionally had attended their discussion meetings.

In reading and analysing the *Tales of Power* books, Chris felt a further sense of recognition that there were indeed definite forces at work within the Universe, with which he was not personally in touch, but which he sensed were undesirable. This instinct, Chris believed, had been so clearly vindicated through Andrew's terrifying experiences of demonic possession.

It was this acknowledgement of an evil spirit, a power of darkness, that was to force for him the issue of whether there was a God; in giving credence to the Devil, Chris reasoned, he had to recognize that a good spirit also existed.

Even so, it was hard for him to give much consideration to such spiritual, ethereal matters when life had dealt such a cruel blow; the reality was too much a matter of cold, hard fact to countenance such notions. Embittered and angry then, Chris' personal dilemma divorced him from any comfort that may otherwise have been derived from maintaining a faith in God.

Only in the tussle with Andrew's demoniacal possession, during that long night of direct confrontation, did he experience a vibrant and powerful life force within himself that was so demonstrably capable of vanquishing evil. It was a strength he had never known before and one which was to leave him questioning much that was apparently intangible, yet which seemed to contain an unlimited potency.

The challenge between Andrew and Cathy, as Eugene, had only heightened his confusion, so that when he and Cathy eventually came to live together the subject of religion was to be the cause of much discussion and argument.

From their first encounter Cathy had professed to being a Buddhist which, given her upbringing among the Chinese, seemed likely enough; it was also a creed with which Chris felt he could cope. Yet in her subsequent challenging of Andrew, Cathy had suddenly produced a strong and undeniable faith in God, and in Christianity, which was clearly her true religion. It came as a bolt from the blue, leaving Chris in utter turmoil; for acknowledging that there was a God made his basic values and moral outlook highly questionable.

Why, he wondered, had Cathy claimed to be a Buddhist when she was actually some kind of Christian? Why had she been afraid to tell him of her real beliefs?

Gradually and haltingly she told him about the visions which had haunted her since childhood. Visions she knew came from God, for she felt it was so and she had always known a close affinity to Him. Cathy showed her bewildered lover the predictions of the Bible, for in the last book, Revelations, was mirrored much that she had seen in her flashes of insight long before she read what it contained. Here was the end of the world as predicted by Jesus and recorded by John on the isle of Patnos; a nasty, violent destruction that would obliterate mankind.

Chris was at once both intrigued and angered; the first because he had always held a deep concern for the future of the human race, a concern he had expressed through socialist politics and later through social work. Now Cathy had shown him a divine plan for the future, and since he could no longer deny the existence of God he was moved to believe in it. Yet he was angered at his helplessness in the face of such inevitable condemnation; and angrily jealous, that God should have given Cathy an insight of such things rather than him. For she had shown no particular regard for her fellows, perhaps hardly surprising given her foreknowledge of the tribulations to come, while he had spent his young life worrying deeply about the way of the world. What was wrong with him that God had not communicated with him sooner? And why, oh why, was he born with the wrong body?

In addition, so vivid and recurrent were Cathy's visions, so attuned was her body both physically and mentally through lengthy meditation, and so confirmed was her faith in God,

171

that the cumulative effect was of a highly sensitive, spiritual being. She was then a complete foil for the disbelieving, and some would argue, a more realistic person than Chris had become. They were a prime example of the platitude that opposites do indeed attract, and it was inevitable that a great deal of each was to rub off on the other.

From then on religion was to become the main turning point of their turbulent life together, the reference for all their subsequent and often recurring anxieties. Chris was essentially a logical person and argued accordingly; Cathy on the contrary was highly illogical, making any rational conclusion virtually impossible, though she tried to provide him with answers. However, nothing she could come up with seemed to Chris to be an ideal and instant solution, and he was enraged and jealous as he had never been in his life.

The anger and envy he had known during his girlhood and which had been levelled usually at men, was something he had been able to handle; for he had been living then in a world without a God, and to some degree it was just bad luck that he'd been born in the wrong body. Now everything was changed, for in recognizing his Maker, there seemed no justification for His maltreatment and neglect, nor for the hideous burden he had been made to carry for more than a quarter of a lifetime.

As yet he had not recognized that God's understanding was always available to all those who believed in Him; and it was only by first coming to see Him in a somewhat unusual light that Chris was eventually to find reassurance and relief.

Indeed to both Chris and Cathy God was to become an entity in which male and female combined, for She, as they preferred to view their creator, surely displayed the qualities of both sexes; referring to God only as He was to underestimate Her essential femininity.

Looking at the Bible, and reading the scriptures helped to clarify their new understanding, as it became apparent that the Old Testament represented God in His masculine role: the warmongering man of dust as depicted through Moses. This seemed to them to ignore the gentle passivity and compassionate nature of God, as exemplified in Jesus Christ and the New Testament; qualities attributable to Her femininity. Having thus recognized the masculine and the feminine in their Maker it seemed logical to the couple that God was able to control

172

the balance of these qualities in all human life. Now they were able to see God as part of their very being, directing and guiding their every motivation.

Not that the couple saw this as offering an excuse for their overwhelming desire to change sex, although it could feasibly be argued that it was a way of easing their guilt. Indeed they felt that this was hardly a contentious issue as there was much in Christian writings and teaching to defend their beliefs.

Nowhere do the scriptures preclude anyone from altering their sex, only bearing reference to a man not wearing women's clothing and vice versa. If transsexuals are to be condemned by Christians and indeed by anyone, for desiring to rectify mistakes that Nature has made with their bodies, then Chris and Cathy believe that certain assumptions need to be challenged.

One popular assumption, that transsexualism is a sexual perversion and that tampering with sexual organs is to defile a divinely formed body, wrongly presumes that sexual gratification is the transsexual's ulterior motive. In fact, the couple insist that sexual gratification means nothing when you have the inner knowledge that the world is making a grave mistake about your own identity. Therefore changing one's outward appearance is of paramount importance, something which can hardly be deemed "a perversion", but rather the repair of what is an overwhelming physical handicap.

Chris and Cathy stoutly maintain that if they believed that altering their bodies was in any way defying God, it is something they would not contemplate. Yet their faith has told them cate-gorically that this is not so. For through Jesus, God showed us the value of compassion; healing the sick and insane, indeed physically transforming the bodies of those who suffered. Can we, therefore, believe that He condemns transsexuals, knowing as He must the misery, the mental and physical frustrations experienced by those trapped within the wrong body?

Surely not, venture Chris and Cathy; for Christ also warned that we cannot hope to understand all that happens to us in life and, furthermore, through the gospel of St Matthew, spoke of sexual relationships, even of eunuchs, advising Christians to accept, rather than to condemn. To make harsh judgements then, without full understanding, is to be condemned ourselves. Accepting this viewpoint, and accepting too that ultimately only God can sit in judgement, means that no one can self-righteously "judge" those who in some way differ from the accepted norm. For how is anyone to know what is and what is not God's will?

Indeed Chris and Cathy now firmly believe that what has happened and is about to happen is all part of God's will, and that however difficult and, at times, obscure, His will remains the guiding light of life.

In recognition of this belief, and long before they decided to take any positive action towards crossing over, they began to study the Bible, to try to discover how God works within the frail framework of humanity. God was no longer to be feared, for He was continually watching over them as they agonized over their decision; ensuring that they recognized the difference between good and evil. It opened their eyes too, to the evils of modern life – to starvation, hatred, murder and racial prejudice.

All this is not to suggest that, in relying on God's support, the couple found any quick or easy solutions. For in those early days before crossing over, Chris in particular found that the agony of being trapped within a woman's body often evoked angry and passionate feelings in him against the Lord. Thoughts he put to paper in revealing verse:

Why do I now have a woman's body,
What has happened to my own.
Is it Your wish that I become a nursemaid now? The great and noble warrior now rears children
How quaint.
Child-minding is such a soothing occupation for a warrior.
But wait, the women cry,
There is nothing wrong with children.
I agree.
There is nothing wrong with children.
But there is something wrong with me.
We look after children all the time, they say.
It won't hurt you for a while.
Physically maybe not.
Physical wounds are not the only things that hurt though.
Physical blows I am used to
Mental stripes are far more painful.
The Lord may have changed my body
But in Her infinite wisdom She did not change my mind.
My temperament remains intact.

174

I am a male imprisoned in a female body
A life sentence.
What was my crime?

Often unable to communicate to Cathy the full import of his frustrations, Chris was to return time and again to a one-sided correspondence with his Creator, whom he was beginning to regard as God and yet with whom the quarrel over his identity was by no means over.

You take away my pride
My manhood gone, what use am I?
What joys can I experience now?
What happiness can be mine?
What do You give me in return, oh great and wonderful one?
A woman's body.
How nice
How practical
I can do a lot with this.
My friends will really like me now.
Where is our comrade they will ask.
That great and noble warrior,
Our friend and champion, where has he gone?
What strange fate has befallen him?
My friends, fate is strange indeed
You would not recognize me now
I have a woman's body.
My fate is hard to hear.
I dare not let you know me now for fear you will want me
And I will not be wanted in a woman's way.
It sickens me.
No more can I be your friend
No more your comrade,
I have been taken to the other side
And I cannot even speak to you.
I am so ashamed I could die.
I would die
Rather death than your laughter,
Rather death than your eyes desiring me.
I was once your friend
No more.
I am very sad.
I am also angry with my God.

175

Very angry.

That anger was to simmer and boil over as the tussle and heartache of his love for Elizabeth ended in her finishing the affair. It was the culmination of months of torment and in the days that followed their irrevocable decision he was to write furious and bitter words to God, whom he felt had surely forsaken him:

From the very beginning You spoilt my life
It could have been good.
Anger and resentment are locked inside
Sometimes I wonder what is beyond my resentment
But most times I hang on to it, not wishing to explore.
If I let go what will happen?
You spoilt my life
I want You to know that.
I want it to hurt You because you hurt me.
There was no need for You to hurt me
But You did it.
What did I do to You?
Nothing as far as I know
And yet You still spoil my life.
Thank You for nothing.

Enraged beyond reason at the seeming hopelessness of his situation, both with Cathy and now with Elizabeth, Chris resorted to cynicism:

...Are we just toys,
Divine playthings to relieve Your boredom?
I do believe we are.
You give us minds but manipulate us
You give us hearts and then break them one by one,
Do we amuse You Lord?
Do our vain struggles against Your might give You pleasure.
You must have the biggest ego in the whole of creation.
I wish I could take You down a peg or two,
Instead its the other way around.
I don't like that.
You make me angry.
You frustrate me.
I kick against You and hurt myself.
Am I a simpleton?
Sometimes I wish You had never created me

Because I don't know why You did.

In the end God, as Perfect Woman, bore the brunt of Chris' rage, while at the same time it was obvious that he feared ultimate rejection:

You make me angry.
If You weren't so beautiful
I could kill You.
All day long
Your vision haunts me
Out of reach
Your sweet voice taunts me.
You make me so angry.
How I've longed to make You mine –
But You are far beyond my mind.
I can't cope with Your perfection;
All I feel is your rejection.

Although these outpourings obviously exhausted him, as the week wore on so the discourse proved therapeutic, his wrath gradually subsiding. Little by little, Cathy began to rebuild his faith and by drawing once again on the Bible, Chris managed to re-affirm his religious beliefs and thereby concentrate once more on their joint venture.

The traumatic summer of 1979 also brought fresh optimism; for Cathy was now on the threshold of womanhood, her body subtly transformed into female contours, her breasts surprisingly firm and rounded, her hips filling out, and with the aid of careful dieting, her gut notably reduced. The possibility of Emma growing up to face two distinctly masculine parents seemed to have passed and the way was clear for Chris to begin treatment.

Chris' monthly injections of testosterone were to prove remarkably effective, far more so than Dr. K had predicted. For as Cathy had scaled down in size, grown weaker, so Chris found himself rapidly gaining in weight and strength. Within eight weeks of beginning his treatment Chris began to sprout facial hair, a growth he immediately shaved and which soon grew stronger. Perhaps surprisingly, he did not feel it to be the cause of great excitement.

'I was more contented than anything, it felt perfectly natural, just right, for everything female was now totally alien to me; as a man I accepted the beard as perfectly normal.'

So responsive was he to the hormones that within four

months the dosage was more than doubled and with it the effects. His voice deepened satisfactorily, which meant that socializing was something he no longer feared.

As his body readily adjusted to its new form, so Chris began to feel much more sure of himself and his quarrel with God burned itself out, only to be replaced by such a feeling of remorse for his bitter outbursts, that once again he took up his writings. This time the tone was startlingly different, for now that he'd rediscovered what it meant to believe, he not only yearned for forgiveness, but wished to know more and more about his faith. The style was verbose, florid in its idolatry, but was undoubtedly a sincere reflection of his feelings at that time.

Lord, I wish to know more of You.
Mistress, I wish to learn to love You deeply.
Only You can give me this knowledge, Lord,
Only You can help me in my search for life
For I do not live at the moment, I exist.
I shall go on existing in this terrible world until such time,
My Lord, as You help me to know You and then I shall live.
God, have pity on me.

Plaintively he begged God's love in discourses which ran many pages long. To Chris, absolute peace of mind was something he had to find within himself, with God's help, rather than by turning to others for assistance. Thus he wrote:

How can I persuade You, Lord to talk to me,
What entreaties must I make?
How can I persuade You Lord, to visit me,
I am so alone without You.
Your voice could comfort me;
Your presence would calm me.
I would be complete.
Now I am empty;
I have a void within my soul which will be filled
Only at Your pleasure.

The imagery Chris invoked was powerfully and sometimes, perhaps unconsciously interwoven with their predicament; and always God was addressed as a bisexual force:

Oh God of Creation, the most perfect being,
The most perfect woman and the most perfect man.
We were created in Your image, Lord, man and woman.
You created us.

Woman and man we are, Lord, and if we would but submit
To Your rule, we would no longer hate one another,
We could live in peace . . .
Please, Lord and Mistress, hear my prayer, for I love You.

Hundreds of words then, numerous pages, were to flow from Chris to God; written prayers, letters, poems, defining his innermost doubts, clarifying the way he and Cathy, indeed the whole of mankind, were to go forward into the future.

The exercise acted as a form of purgative; and while the equation even now remains unsolved, the new reliance Chris could place on God made life infinitely more bearable.

As the whole religious question continued to penetrate their daily life together, so did their plan to cross over. As their bodies continued to change at a rapid rate, their emotional development could hardly keep pace and every day they seemed to be faced with a barrage of fresh questions and problems.

Now that he had given up work, Chris found himself increasingly bored with the monotony of home life, cooped up in a place where there was no room for individual privacy, no escape from either the clutter of Emma's play or Cathy's incessant chatter. Yet if there was not much of a practical nature with which to occupy his time, there was nonetheless a great need for mental deliberation; for neither of them had eased up on the strict programme of self-analysis.

Both were reluctant to resort to the help of psychiatrists or psychologists, or any other so-called experts on all sexual and mental problems; for they felt sensitive that as transsexuals they might well be misjudged, and out of ignorance wrongly diagnosed as some kind of fetishists.

It was unfortunate if not surprising that the couple were suspicious of outside help, as some of the doctors they had sought assistance from so far had been sparing with their offers of support. While it was vital to keep on the good side of the doctors so that drugs would continue to be prescribed and surgery could be pressed for, Chris and Cathy had given up expecting anything approaching sympathy from some of the medical profession.

'On the one hand we both had a certain mistrust of them as regards our psychological needs. On the other, while we were eternally grateful for their accepting us as patients, it was frightening to be taking such large amounts of drugs without

179

any reassurance that we weren't doing irreparable damage to our health.

'No one seemed to question what was going on in our minds as a result of all this; it was as if our emotions could take care of themselves, and hang the side effects; as if they had no desire to get involved, almost as if they were embarrassed by the whole thing.

'In fact it sometimes seemed that they were giving us the treatment simply to satisfy our silly little minds, as if it'd keep us quiet. And always they were warning us not to expect anything to happen, when quite clearly we were changing radically in every way.'

This apparent lack of genuine concern was reinforced when Cathy next went up to London to see the doctor. During her brief, early morning appointment the nonchalance shown to her by the consultant may well have been part of a complex professional approach aimed at inducing from her nothing but the truth, but it hardly inspired confidence; on the contrary, it made the ordeal all the more unnerving. So pronounced now were her breasts that the doctor appeared quite astonished.

'He said "What have you got in there?", expecting me to say I'd padded myself up with socks. When I said breasts, and they're all my own, he said "Good God! And before breakfast too." I asked him if he wanted to have a look, because I'd expected he'd want to examine me, but he didn't want to know.'

If it was an abrasive fifteen minutes it did at least elicit the promise of further treatment with new medication from the Continent. The doctor was vague, but he did not give the impression that an operation was out of the question. 'It was as if the only way to get there was to play this man's game, to never be anything but polite, not to ask too many questions but to answer his, however difficult and antagonistic he decided to be. It was awful and I always came home in a dreadful state, there was so much I'd wanted to ask but daren't mention. The only consolation was that everyone dependent on his help was treated in the same way.'

If Chris and Cathy were left feeling like some kind of curious medical guinea pigs, who didn't deserve to be treated like proper human beings, theirs is, after all, a subjective viewpoint and perhaps a little unfair on the doctors faced with a medical and psychological problem that science is still struggling to understand. However, the last thing Cathy and Chris would do is to falsify the facts, for antagonizing the medical profession would hardly be the best tactics for obtaining much-wanted surgery. They have now learned to cope with what they see as something of a cat and mouse game, for the only way they will be able to achieve their ultimate goal is by not allowing themselves to become upset along the way. They feel that if they had sufficient money to obtain surgery privately things might be different, for then many of the constraints and obstacles they face would disappear. Doctors have been hesitant to encourage such drastic treatment without first satisfying themselves that Chris and Cathy's case was genuine, and therefore the onus of spending National Health resources on such patients fell heavily on the couple; the cost of a total sex change operation is estimated at around ten thousand pounds. For Chris and Cathy it would, of course, cost twice that amount, and given their scant income and the likelihood that they would soon be utterly dependent on state benefits, a private operation was out of the question. Yet so rapid was Chris' transformation to manhood that his chest was now a constant embarrassment. He looked and felt totally incongruous and, while he had been strapping himself tight with bandages for months, flattening and crushing his breasts was painful, not to say a restriction on his breathing.

A total mastectomy seemed the answer and, even if it took the last of their savings from the sale of the house and his salary too, the couple decided it was worth the sacrifice. It was unlikely that he could have the surgery on the Health Service; for one thing there were long waiting lists for such operations, with priority rightly given to women suffering from breast cancer.

So, that November, Chris booked himself into a private clinic and with their last five hundred pounds said goodbye to his breasts forever. The clinic was discreet and there was no suggestion of disapproval at what he was undertaking; for, as he had reckoned, money talked. The atmosphere was one of cool efficiency, of impersonal yet strict application to ensure that the job was properly done, and for that Chris was grateful.

He was left feeling very sore, but the scarring was minimal and more than compensated for by the psychological fillip of having successfully undertaken this first major step.

Cathy too was feeling a new confidence, for she had been

undergoing speech therapy to improve the pitch and tone of her voice. Painfully conscious of how she sounded to others, she now enunciated clearly, if for a while rather unnaturally, first thinking through what she had to say and then, more importantly, how to say it. It was a noticeable improvement, although there were times, particularly when she was under stress, when she found her voice automatically deepening. Despite all this, she was still reticent whenever they ventured out together, happy to let Chris take the initiative. By now they had learned to judge whether or not they would be accepted by certain company and mixed accordingly, for the hormone treatment did much to heighten their sensitivities and the slightest upset took an inordinately long time to overcome. It was, as they had expected, as if they were trying to recapture the excitement of being teenagers, their punk friends continuing to provide an outlet for unsophisticated enjoyment. Mixing with youngsters, some of whose parents were Chris and Cathy's contemporaries, they revelled in the gang-like atmosphere of camaraderie, the casual friendships which made few demands, the unpredictability of nights spent wandering the town with an ebullient crowd of very individual people, who, dressed to kill, had few cares or worries and an overall naivety that made it possible to believe that anything could be achieved. It was important, however, to gain a street credibility, a far easier task for Cathy than for Chris, who was known to be a social worker and thereby on the fringes of the Establishment.

Cathy, clearly the more flamboyant of the two, endeared herself to the younger girls who took to calling her Eve; it was a strangely evocative choice for someone whom womanhood had eluded for so long.

Even so, it took Cathy many months to feel at ease with her friends, for the extrovert that Cathy had become as Sifu Lung had diminished along with her strength and for a long time she tended to hide behind Chris, for when she was with him she felt safe, not needing to say much for herself. But in order to develop, it was essential that she mix with women of whatever age or inclination, for only by being with them would she learn their ways and finally become integrated as a person in her own right.

Exasperated at her reluctance to show any independence, Chris literally resorted to forcing Cathy out of the door, making her join the other girls at the local pub while he babysat with Emma. Two or three times a week she would be sent out for this valuable therapy, a move which gradually proved successful. It was never easy, for the pub was also a skinhead haunt and Cathy lived in fear of being approached, as a number of the girls often were. Her voice would surely falter, revealing her fading masculinity. 'I was so afraid that I'd get my head bashed in if they took me for some sort of queer, I was always extremely nervous.' There remained the ever-perplexing problem of using the toilet, for there was always the nagging fear of being challenged at the doorway. For the most part Chris and Cathy's anxiety was unwarranted although Chris still limited his drinking to avoid the need of relieving himself. He naturally headed straight for the gents' cubicles, but many were without locks.

'I used to put my hand against the door and hope that no one would burst in.' Fortunately there was only one potentially embarrassing incident, when he found himself in the ladies by mistake. Three girls fixing their hair, stared in amazement at this man in their midst. 'I made my apologies and left.' Chris considered the girls' bewilderment something of a compliment.

If Cathy was beginning to find her feet and thereby to rebuild her self-confidence, it was infinitely harder for Chris, for mixing with men in their somewhat enclosed society was a real test of his courage; their experience was so totally at variance with his own that finding common ground proved exceptionally difficult. Striking up any lasting male friendships is something that Chris had not really been able to achieve, even now, yet it is something he has craved since childhood. While he is obviously grateful to the punk fraternity for its friendliness and easy acceptance of both Cathy and himself, he still sometimes feels the need for the intellectual stimulus of the company of men of his own age.

Nevertheless, there was no doubting that men were beginning to accept him as one of their own kind and to react accordingly. Once, when jumping on the wrong bus by mistake he momentarily reverted to the feminine wile of smiling sweetly at the driver – in the hope that he would stop – the usual male reaction of showing sympathy he had experienced as Anne was not forthcoming; instead, the driver swore at Chris' incompetence!

'I prefer it the way it is now of course, but it's been a shock, after twenty eight years of males being basically nice to you because of what they thought you were, now its totally different, they're far more aggressive. It's as if beforehand they weren't being pleasant to you as a person in your own right, but as a woman. Now they're much more direct.'

So it was by way of much self criticism, determined effort and careful planning that the couple managed to make steady and pleasing progress; never rushing impetuously ahead of what minds and bodies could contend with at any given time. If they had any preconceived ideas of how complex crossing over might be, then the reality proved far slower and more painstaking than they had ever imagined. For Cathy the loss of her body strength and the corresponding lassitude came as an unpleasant surprise; yet she recognized its value in attaining her goal of total femininity, but it was only after a long period of rationalization that she was finally able to accept that this was indeed the price she had to pay.

With such large and regular doses of hormones bombarding their systems, it was only a matter of months before both Cathy and Chris became infertile. For Cathy the inability to perform any longer as a man was a welcome relief, for her shrinking genitals no longer seemed so obtrusive. For Chris the eventual cessation of his menstrual periods was a cause for some celebration.

Since their first experience of physical intimacy they had automatically adopted opposite sexual roles and in making love had used their bodies, as best they could, accordingly. So that when they physically began to change, it was of little consequence; far more disturbing and naturally frustrating, was the gradual loss of feeling in the erogenous zones which for some considerable time made sexual fulfilment an impossibility. Living in a sexual limbo, a no man's land where their bodies were dulled of sensation, as though deliberately courting impotence, they needed more than ever to draw on their dual strength of purpose.

If it were not for the fact that they were sharing the ordeal they would have stood little chance of enduring this most challenging stage of the transformation, for their sexual neutrality in no way stifled their natural urges and desires.

'We muddled through as best we could, loving each other in

our limited way, hoping against hope that it wouldn't last and comforting one another with the thought that things had to get worse before they could get better.'

How much worse they had never imagined; for the doctors had specified that in order to receive medical treatment the couple would have to conduct themselves with utmost propriety and discretion during their changeover, revealing to no one other than the immediate family what they were about to do. They had agreed to this willingly, for they had no desire to risk losing the doctors' cooperation, nor to expose themselves unnecessarily to scandal.

It therefore came as a shock that a social security clerk – who had encountered the couple when they collected the weekly state benefit that was now their only income – saw fit to mention them in conversation at a local pub.

The suspicion that there was something odd about the pair was soon picked up by an over-eager journalist, and in no time at all a somewhat garbled and vague account of their story was splashed across the front page of the city's evening newspaper. No names were mentioned, the details inaccurate; while the public read the tale with interest, little further thought could have been given to it; the anonymity of the couple concerned prevented the story from having any lasting impression at that stage.

But unfortunately Fleet Street seized upon the story, seeing it as a sensational true-life drama that ought to be exposed before the eager curiosity of the reading public. Tracking down this bizarre family became a top priority and a journalist with a reputation for seeking out the impossible was dispatched from London on the unenviable task of foot slogging around Handsworth in search of Britain's, and possibly the world's, first transsexual couple.

Unknown to Chris and Cathy, who were already sick with worry over the effects on their doctors of the original story, the hunt was well and truly on. Publicity was the very last thing they wanted or needed; their crossing over and their family life could only be misinterpreted, or worse, grossly distorted into something obscene and deviant. Naively, it had never occurred to them that they were particularly extraordinary, worthy of the interest to the public and the national press.

It is a measure of their success in keeping themselves very

much to themselves that it took the intrepid reporter a week of exhaustive and exhausting legwork to find them; not even Chris and Cathy's immediate neighbours had guessed the truth about the young couple in their midst.

Cathy and Chris were, nonetheless, caught momentarily off their guard, for the lapse in time since the story first broke had given them a measure of false confidence. However, they were deeply disturbed by this invasion of their privacy and, in no uncertain terms, told the bloodhound from Fleet Street what he could do with his questions. But the journalist was not to be dissuaded by such a trifling inconvenience as the couple's lack of cooperation; circuitous inquiry had given him enough information to write a story infinitely more substantial than the one that had first appeared in the local press and, by the next morning, Chris and Cathy's story had become breakfast reading in households throughout the country.

Appalled by the revelations which, baldly stated in print, allowed no room for proper explanation of their feelings, the couple felt exploited and vulnerable, and tried to bolt themselves apart from the world outside their home. For the next forty-eight hours they were held under siege as the country's national press journalists set up camp outside the house in pursuit of the serious quest of getting to the bottom of the transsexual story.

The masculine aggression that Chris had felt more conscious of as his treatment progressed now welled up as never before; both he and Cathy felt furious at this development and terrified of the repercussions that it might have on their treatment. What on earth would the doctors say? What of Chris' family, which all the time had been kept in ignorance of the fact that their daughter was seeking to become a man? Of less immediate concern, but still worrying was the effect that their sudden notoriety might have on their new-found friends and neighbours. How were they going to be able to face the people around them now that their misfortune was a topic of heated public discussion?

19

Despite the couple's refusal to answer questions or to be turned into a circus act, the press stoically sat it out, believing that siege tactics would have to prove successful eventually. Chris and Cathy could not remain locked inside forever. Offers of substantial sums of money to tell the full story were pushed under the door but none was to bear fruit. Every ruse was employed to get at the facts; a particularly ruthless pair of reporters plied May Brown with whisky until she was drunk and loose of tongue. She told them of Eugene's childhood, his fondness for dressing in women's clothes, the couple's love for each other and their daughter, Emma. By the time this account appeared their fame was spreading and the pressure growing unbearable. Anxious to set the record straight they finally agreed to talk to a reporter from a Wolverhampton paper and were relieved at the accuracy and sympathetic treatment of the subsequent report. Amongst all the offers of payment this was one they were to accept and even that only after some hesitation; it seemed a denigration of all they were striving for, but somehow a payment of fifty pounds hardly seemed to signify corruption and such were their financial circumstances that, on balance, it seemed nonsensical to return the cheque.

Still reeling from the shock of discovery, they were visited by journalists from Europe, by television film crews from Brazil and, more perturbing, from Birmingham itself. Finally they agreed to a televised interview, assured that there would be no edits and that the interview would run for a full seven minutes. They welcomed the opportunity to give their version at first hand, yet were full of misgivings at putting a visual image to the names with which by now the public had become familiar. Yet

187

on balance they decided it was expedient, if only for their own sanity, to satisfy the public curiosity in a way which presented as accurate a picture as possible of their dilemma, in the hope that the clamour for more information would quickly burn itself out.

In the end, although the interview went well and the TV company kept all their promises and portrayed them in a sympathetic light, Cathy and Chris came to regret that they'd agreed to it at all. They had been exposed to a public unable to cope with the idea of transsexualism and, as a result, their carefully nurtured self-confidence evaporated virtually overnight; to venture out, as they had begun to do so freely, now seemed an impossibility, for they felt themselves wide open to ridicule and contempt and feared greatly for the impact this would have on little Emma.

Yet above all these troubles there was one overriding consideration: the London consultant, on whom so much of their future happiness depended, had been adamant that treatment could only continue if the utmost secrecy was maintained, if their lives remained essentially private. That criterion had clearly been abused and despite a desperate letter from Cathy explaining their innocence in the whole affair, their worst fears were realized. In a curt response, the consultant advised them that he was terminating his involvement in their case; Cathy could no longer remain his patient and against that there could be no appeal.

After the anguish and torment that life had brought them, this was a bitter irony. To have been robbed of her chance of attaining complete womanhood by something not of her wish or doing was a staggering blow to Cathy and one from which they both have yet to recover completely.

Time was of the essence; Emma was growing up fast and they had to complete their transformations before she was old enough to feel that Mummy and Daddy were in any way not "normal". Now they were facing a severe setback, not only at a loss to know where to turn for surgical help, but also so unnerved by the prospect that their progress might be hampered.

It was a natural reaction to their depression that they should withdraw into themselves, mistrustful, angry, hurt and fearful of further recriminations.

It was only after several months had passed by that Chris

managed to convince Cathy of the need to continue her social therapy; although it took her several abortive trips to find the courage to confront her friends.

'I told him I'd been to the clubs or to the pub but instead I'd just wander down the road and hide for a while and then come home.'

It took the encouragement of a punk acquaintance, who saw her hanging around obviously at a loose end, to finally take the plunge and re-establish her friendships. As it transpired there was much friendly curiosity but little animosity, for the punks were above all generous in their acceptance of all that was unusual and beyond the norm.

For Chris' family to learn the truth about their daughter through all the publicity was an immeasurable shock, and one from which even now they have not fully recovered. Although Chris had deliberately avoided telling his family the truth, he never anticipated that they would have to learn it in such a brutal and dispassionate way; now it would be far harder to break down the barrier that had built up between them, as he had one day hoped to do. Although it was obvious that they were suffering deeply as a result of all this Chris now felt so uncertain of himself that coping with any additional distress was for the moment out of the question.

The couple felt marooned, for while the hormone treatment continued, so their respective masculinity and femininity grew more pronounced; Cathy in particular felt more than ready for the cosmetic surgery. 'It was as if I felt entirely feminine in every respect; I now felt just like a woman, I reacted instinctively like a woman and I looked like one. Every pore in my skin seemed to be oozing with it, but I needed to lose my private parts, they were the only things that felt wrong. It wasn't even so much that I had to look right, but because of them, emotionally I felt incomplete.' Cathy feared that as her penis became atrophied and left as a virtually useless appendage, it could somehow become infected; a fear which may have been groundless, but one which frequently preyed on her mind.

Instinctively then, she felt herself ready to take the final step and yet as the probability of obtaining her operation became more remote, she grew more and more anxious. Living now in a permanent state of nervous tension, she found it impossible to stay calm for long.

189

For without the final surgery she and Chris seemed doomed to remain like two chimeras, an unimaginable horror. Eventually to everyone's surprise it was a combination of this bitter frustration and the unwelcome publicity, that gave Cathy the resolve to fight back. For once the dread of being labelled as freaks had subsided and she accepted that their secret was out, Cathy's attitude became philosophical.

There was no option other than to make the best of it and in a perverse way the glimpse of once more being in the limelight – something she had not enjoyed since the glorious height of her Kung Fu days – had wetted her appetite.

'I was always something of an exhibitionist underneath it all, I loved the excitement of showmanship, of being dramatic and theatrical in my performance. Now I decided that I'd show them I wasn't afraid, that I was proud of being a woman and if people weren't prepared to accept me for what I was, then it was just too bad.'

Although this was a positive sign of her growing maturity from girl into woman there were, even so, inevitable lapses when she was overcome by despair; and the struggle to let herself go and to thereby act entirely on her own feelings is something that still continues to this day.

'Chris complains that I still can't totally respect my own feelings and so be the wholly natural person he sees in me. If I could then I'd be more feminine than I already am, but it's hard to have that confidence.'

Despite these niggling doubts, Cathy began to take the initiative in developing friendships, to join her girlfriends for regular night outs, dressing with a flamboyance in clothes she made herself. She experimented with her hair, dying it an assortment of outlandish shades, backcombing it into the wildly abandoned look favoured by the young punks. It was a delicious indulgence, a rebellious adolescent gesture of defiance in the face of the doctor's rejection, the public's unyielding scrutiny.

As he had dispensed much of his energy and willpower on supporting Cathy through their ordeal, Chris had little left for bolstering up his own confidence. By nature the more introvert of the two, he found it infinitely harder to come to terms with what he could only regard as a calamity. Given his continuing debate with God and the degree to which everything preyed upon his mind, it was little wonder that he became acutely depressed:

'I'd concentrated so much on helping Cathy get straightened out again that I hadn't had time to think about myself. The most important thing was to see our plan through, but it seemed as if everything was conspiring against us, that no one really cared what happened; there were times when I began to despair.'

It was one of their blackest periods; the year that had augered so well had turned sour, for they had little money and now that their story was known, no likelihood of ever earning any. No way then, of repairing their broken cooker, of making their home more comfortable; no means of escape from one another's company twenty-four hours a day; no hope of operations and with that, no certain future. If the situation seemed hopeless and themselves helpless to improve it, then that was the price of notoriety.

Throughout her parents' ordeal, Emma remained the one bright spark in their lives. What of the child born of this unique love match? How was she faring in such hapless times? What was the justification of bringing her into a world where her mother and father were unlike any other and where she would be open to hurt and to ridicule of the worst kind?

One thing can be said categorically: the decision to conceive a child of their relationship was not one Chris and Cathy made lightly. Apart from Chris' abhorrence of pregnancy and childbirth, the couple realized that their child would be instantly vulnerable and they never for one moment underestimated the special care and attention that would be needed to protect her during her formative years.

Hence the careful preparations, the timing of their treatment to avoid her confusion, the daily routine of an early morning playtime with Chris, while Cathy prepared herself and her face for her daughter's eyes. For Emma has never seen her parents undressed, her mother without makeup, has never witnessed conversations in which their predicament was discussed.

So it is that the little girl has grown up shielded as far as possible from the truth about her parents and loving them for what they are to her. To see them together is no weird, erroneous experience, for so naturally does Cathy take the role of her mother and Chris her father, that to hear Emma refer to them as such and react accordingly comes as no surprise. It is this total acceptance on the part of all three that inspires a basis of confidence in the future.

Her parents feel strongly that Emma Johnson Lung is a well-balanced child, secure and happy as a result of parental love and that there is no reason to suppose that she will not be able to enjoy a normal upbringing and adolescence. Chris and Cathy certainly feel a deep commitment to their daughter's future.

The couple's argument is clear:

'A lot of families have handicaps in one way or another and we are really no different to other handicapped people. If someone's physically deformed, do you tell them they can't have a child? Don't we have the same rights to love and nurture a child as anyone else?'

If that sounds ostensibly selfish then it is resoundingly vindicated by their love for little Em, who enjoys the full time attentions of both her parents, as well as that of her maternal grandparents.

A bright, talkative affectionate little soul, she mixes happily in company and shows a vivid imagination in her play. It is in that one area that for a while she suffered, because, after the publicity, Cathy fought shy of mixing with other mothers and of introducing Emma to a playgroup. At three and a half, she obviously needed the company of other children of a similar age, but for a while this just was not possible.

Once that barrier had been overcome, Cathy was relieved to find no mention made of her own condition, rather an instant friendliness from all concerned. It was to be the making of young Emma, for the playleaders found her delightfully outgoing and completely lacking in the usual initial shyness. Missing a day's play session makes her miserable; she is at her happiest among her little friends, playing and painting bright, busy pictures which hang like a gallery on the living room wall. In every respect then, Emma is more at one with herself and her little world than many children who have the misfortune to be born into unstable homes or of unhappy marriages.

That is not to say that the responsibilities of parenthood sit in an entirely straightforward manner on Chris and Cathy. For while the status of being parents has afforded them a social stance which has made crossing over a little easier, having to cope with a young daughter at this stage in their lives is no enviable task and they have to come to terms with their roles on these two different levels.

For Cathy, her child remains a constant loving factor in life and one for which she feels a total responsibility.

'I enjoy being her mother, it's something I know I can cope with and even if I couldn't get life sorted out my way, I'd still feel responsible for her and would have to consider her first and foremost.

'Yet I still feel that on my other emotional level I need to have a pretty wild youth, I need to go out and enjoy myself in that way. What I have to ensure is that it doesn't interfere with Emma; and I think that with Chris' help, there's no reason why I shouldn't be able to do both.'

For Chris too, his unquestionable love for Emma is countered by his emotional immaturity as a man.

'Sometimes I feel towards her like a kid myself, like someone who's got someone pregnant while very young and finds himself still trapped at twenty. It's like the natural resentment of any young fellow caught in those circumstances and sometimes the responsibility gets me down. But I could never desert her, could never imagine life without her now.'

It is Emma then, who provides a stability in their family life together and for whom they are eternally grateful; but what of the years to come?

She will soon reach school age and Chris and Cathy recognize that it is then her problems could start; they had striven to complete their changeover before Emma is old enough to understand or be exposed to the lack of understanding of others, to move away with Emma to start a new life elsewhere, where their background would be unknown and they could tell her the truth in their own way, when the moment was right.

The publicity has put a stop to all that and the problem of how to handle Emma has now become more pressing. Yet her parents share an inner confidence that their darling daughter will one day understand and in so doing, with their support, find the strength of character to cope.

'We want her to grow up feeling free, but never cheated or deserted. She knows we'll always love her and that we'll never give up on her; now we can only hope and pray that she'll accept us, and somehow, we feel sure she will.'

193

20

Comparatively little about transsexualism has been written, or for that matter researched; for, until 1949 the condition was not even named and before 1953 no authoritative paper on the subject had been published.

It is by its very nature at once an intriguing yet potentially dangerous condition for the medical profession; a spectacular disorder, it brings uncertainty to the definitions of perversion, challenges classic theories and frustrates the psychoanalysts, for no transsexual has ever had their feelings modified or "cured". Furthermore, it forces physicians into the unenviable position of flouting the law in encouraging a patient to change sex and to be recognized in that new identity, so alien to their original birth certificate.

As ethically there is some debate regarding the use of hormones and surgery to change the anatomy there is little wonder that the medical world has fought shy of widespread involvement.

So unexplored is the transsexuals' world that while presumably rare, no one is sure how uncommon the condition is, for as yet there is no firm agreement as to who exactly qualifies to be called a transsexual.

These are just some of the thoughts of Dr Robert Stoller the one man who has attempted to make any lengthy study of transsexualism; a psychoanalyst of world repute and a specialist in the treatment of problems of gender identity.

Few would disagree that men and women have at one time arisen out of a common interest, which still lives on in the bisexual anlage in all humans. They have differentiated in the course of development without ever being completely separated from one another. So that in the psychological make-up of the individual, the two components, male and female, must be linked in harmony.

What prescribes the destiny of those trapped within the wrong body, living as they do inside an invisible prison? What causes this deviance of identity that manifests itself at a very early age, much earlier than the different conditions that are considered unconventional or perverse sexual tendencies? It seems clear that the notion of being born in the wrong body occurs to the young child with such conviction that Stoller describes it as "the fundamental of personality" that is most unaltered by any experience to come.

Some would argue that it is a genetic disorder, others that it is due to a hormonal defect, created by the mother taking prenatal cross-sexed drugs, which in some way affect the organization of her baby's brain during the critical period of foetal development. For at three to four months of gestation, the foetus' biological sexuality is determined, and the basically female embryo remains either unchanged, or develops male characteristics.

As far as transsexuals are concerned, most of these arguments remain unproven; for while there is as yet no way of testing the hormonal levels of a human foetus, there is no categorical proof that such a defect cannot occur.

Neither is there any collated evidence to prove that trans-sexualism is an inherited condition running in families, nor that it usually effects more than one offspring.

Are there any satisfactory explanations?

Certainly transsexuals are not infectious or dangerous, nor do they inflict harm on others; nor is it a psychiatric illness rather a condition that only the patient can cope with for themselves, as Cathy and Chris have found to their cost. While they seek understanding, they have never desired a cure to stop them feeling the way they do.

While Freud himself observed that latent femininity and masculinity are in all of us, that is not sufficient for the transsexual. The sense of core gender identity, or being male or female, is normally derived from three sources: the anatomy and physiology of a person, the attitude of parents and associates towards a child's gender role and a biological force which has the power to modify the forces of a child's environment. It is

196

perhaps the latter, soluble and diffuse that it might be, that has the profoundest influence upon a transsexual, as if tangible existence were challenging the very essence of life and that every empirical fact contains its beyond.

Stoller therefore considers a transsexual to be a person who feels himself, both consciously and unconsciously, to belong to the opposite sex, while at the same time in no way denying his sexual anatomy. For it is, he maintains, the preservation of one's sense of self, not one's anatomical appearance, that determines behaviour; the transsexual therefore longs to change sex so that his or her body will conform to his or her psyche.

Dr Stoller's own theory of the cause, based most particularly on casework, again has no real scientific support, but is none-theless of genuine interest. His further descriptions of what characterizes transsexuality also bears a mention: it is, he says, the only condition in which a person will destroy his or her genitalia and reproductive organs for purely psychological reasons.

Furthermore, in this distortion of reality, on reaching adolescence the transsexual's own body turns against him, for in a male the penis insists on asserting its inescapable maleness, the female's uterus brings about the onset of menstruation, leaving the subject in abject despair.

Stoller remains convinced that the circumstances of the family and parental attitude have much to answer for in per-petuating transsexualism, as a result of the evidence he has collated through clinical trials, but which scientifically have still to be proved or disproved.

Chris and Cathy believe that the explanation is largely biological, for it is within this seemingly incomprehensible area that they have always maintained the roots of their dilemma lie. For they feel that the persistent, nagging doubts they have held since childhood are the result not of social conditioning, rather of a biological malfunction at the time of sexual differentiation within the womb.

The couple agree that in order to come to terms with their problem, they have had to regard it as a physical handicap and in so doing they've rejected psycho-analytical theory. They both feel that handicaps such as theirs coupled with subsequent emotional deprivation during their childhood, can be best overcome if tackled scientifically. Hence their painstaking plan of action, the systematic retracing of emotional development and the need to relive their youth in order to emerge as wholesome, complete adults with assured identities. If their theory is not infallible, they themselves are nonetheless proof of the value of such a course of action and, in the long term, both realize that intensive self-analysis can only help them further in coming to terms with themselves and their situation.

In the absence of conclusive evidence or precise explanation as to how transsexualism occurs, all theories must be welcomed and explored.

Although Dr. Stoller can justifiably claim to be sympathetic towards transsexuals, it nevertheless remains nothing short of scandalous that it is a problem that society has chosen to ignore; that so little is done to guide and counsel those undergoing treatment or that few follow-up reports exist on patients who have completed crossing over. We remain largely ignorant of how these transsexuals fare, whether they suffer postoperative complications, depressions, or indeed how many survive to enjoy the life they have always desired.

So to the present, for as in all true life tales there is rarely a happy ending and this is no exception. With the repercussions of the untimely publicity continuing to reverberate and the final hurdle still to be overcome, as a couple Cathy and Chris remain determined to succeed.

In six years together although much has been achieved against incalculable and unforeseen odds, time after time they have had to stop themselves sinking into the depths of despair. For theirs has been a lonely venture, one in which support has spasmodically been offered, only to fade away under the pressures of social convention.

Only now comes renewed hope of completing their chosen course of obtaining the elusive surgical treatment. For in the light of their doctor's concern at the state of their health, they have again been recommended for consultation. Already during extensive examination, doctors have shown amazement at their response to hormonal treatment and the resulting transformation. In blood and urine tests to measure the body's hormonal levels the diagnosis was favourable; there was too a marked change in body weight, Cathy some two stones lighter than she had been prior to treatment, Chris considerably heavier.

After years of a daily intake ten times the amount of a high dosage birth pill, Cathy is expected to respond well to an oestrogen implant which, in the long term, has fewer corresponding risks. For whether they eventually receive surgery or not, neither of them can ever relinquish their hormone treatment without serious physical regression, and therefore the risks of blood clotting and for Chris, of liver disorders, are a constant factor. He too is awaiting an implant of testosterone; in the meantime he must limit his alcohol intake. After that there is fresh promise of surgery, for they have finally satisfied the medics in the basic criteria generally demanded before crossing over: that they have felt as they do since childhood; that they have lived as one of the opposite chosen sex for two years; and that they are not, by their actions, breaking up a marriage.

So they await the final transformation of their bodies: and yet once again there is a delay, for economic stringencies are hampering the work of the doctors who have now agreed to help. Yet as they wait, further startling progress continues to provide some consolation. For Chris' genitals are changing fast and becoming recognizably male in shape and form, so much so that even the doctors are encouraged.

Even more remarkable is the return of the full sexual feeling and fulfilment; for in achieving orgasm, both maintain they are knowing a new experience, unlike anything they knew before while trapped in the wrong bodies. After some discussion both recognized the other's feelings; for Cathy, the excitement that permeated her whole body Chris knew to be a truly female orgasm, while the far more direct, purposeful force of his own satisfaction was undoubtedly that of a male. It was an intriguing comparison, one that few could ever hope to be fortunate enough to make and furthermore, surely the most intimate substantiation of their real identities.

In continuing to build a solid framework from which they can perceive the rest of the world some things inevitably are still to be achieved, for despite a marked improvement both have still to reach full emotional maturity.

New horizons and new challenges await them, as Cathy prepares to express herself through their music. Encouraged by the initial response to her early musical attempts, she is rehearsing a band to perform the songs she and Chris have recently written. Cathy sees their songs principally as a diversion, a new interest now that they have had to give up martial arts, but they are also a medium of communication for two people who are still withdrawn and sensitive. They like to think that, in their own way, they can help create a better understanding of the problems of transsexualism, and it is this desire that encouraged them to write this book.

New permutations of their extraordinary equation continue to arise, for as well as their mutual love for one another comes the notion of a transsexual bisexual nature. It would be wrong to suppose that their condition precludes individual sexual preference; indeed, as has been seen, bisexuality is thought to be closely interlinked with their transsexualism. A transsexual in his or her true gender may have heterosexual (attracted only to the opposite of their true sex), bisexual (attracted to both sexes), lesbian or homosexual inclinations.

Hence Cathy's interest in other women, an interest in no respect akin to that of a man for a woman, rather that of one woman for another, and one that cannot detract from her love for Chris, as her man.

If it is thus a tangled web we weave, then such is the nature of transsexualism and of this unique story of love and impassioned conviction. In writing it has proved unexpectedly difficult to relive those earlier days of Anne and Eugene, so unpalatable and detestable is the memory. Nor can there be any straight-forward conclusion, for once their ultimate goal is reached, there can be no guarantee that the remainder of their lives will be any improvement on the past. The only certainty is that Chris and Cathy, as man and woman together, and with Emma at their side, will face the world in the way they believe Nature intended, freed from the emotional torment of being born into the wrong bodies.

QUOTED REFERENCES

Page 248 The Lord Desires Our Love From A Solitary Way, James Nisbet and Co. Ltd. 21 Berners St, London (Published well before turn of century)

Biblical References from the Gospel of St Matthew. Chap 19 V12 St Paul, Romans. Chap 2 v1-3